Hapl

William Chadwick was born in Swanage, Dorset. He emigrated to Canada when he was 17. He attended the University of Toronto and then took a Ph.D. at University College, London. On returning to Canada he taught English and Drama at the University of Regina, Saskatchewan and then the University of Waterloo, Ontario. He has published books on the plays of William Wycherley, and Kitchener, Ontario in World War I, has had two plays professionally produced, and published a number of poems. In 2000 he retired to the Somerset Levels, where he lives with his wife and two children.

The Rescue of the Prague Refugees 1938-39

William Chadwick

Matador
5 Weir Road
Kibworth Beauchamp
Leicester LE8 0LQ, UK
Tel: (+44) 116 279 2299
Fax: (+44) 116 279 2277
Email: books@troubador.co.uk
Web: www.troubador.co.uk/matador

ISBN 978 1848765 047

British Library Cataloguing in Publication Data.
A catalogue record for this book is available from the British Library.

Copies of this book may be obtained from the Matador webshop
(http://www.troubador.co.uk/shop.asp) and also from wrchadwick@tiscali.co.uk
£10 plus postage

Typeset in 11pt Palatino by Troubador Publishing Ltd, Leicester, UK
Printed and bound in Great Britain by TJI Digital, Padstow, Cornwall

Matador is an imprint of Troubador Publishing Ltd

In Memoriam

All those who said goodbye at the airport and on the Prague station platforms but who were unable to follow.

For My Wife Who Cannot Be Thanked Enough

15th March 1939

And she said
The Germans have marched into Prague
And she said
THE GER-MANS HAVE MARCHED IN-TO PRAGUE
Careless, eleven,
I smile comprehension
(Or was it embarrassment?
Or was it a not-wanting-to-know?
How can I tell now
So many years later?)
And I wrote in my letter
What are
the German uniforms like?
And my father replying,
(and my father forgiving me):
Not bad
as uniforms go.

Gerda Mayer
(from *Monkey on the Analyst's Couch*)

CONTENTS

PROLOGUE

Accurate scholarship can
Unearth the whole offence
From Luther until now
That has driven a culture mad,
Find what occurred at Linz,
What huge imago made
A psychopathic god.

W.H. Auden, "1ˢᵗ September 1939"

By the middle of the 1930's it was obvious to many people that a wide-ranging European war was on the way. Already the prescient and the moneyed were moving themselves and their households to lands that appeared to be safer. As the decade progressed this steady flow of emigration increased in direct proportion to the bellicosity of the Third Reich. By 1938 the madness of a culture was in full flow. In March of that year Austria was occupied; in September England and France at Munich were reduced to that ancient tactic of political cowardice, once known as danegeld, now named "appeasement"; in October the strange conglomeration of territories around the edge of Czechoslovakia called the Sudetenland were occupied by the German army; November saw the first signs of the coming horror during Kristallnacht; and all the time the face of the psychopath from Linz increasingly monopolized the hoardings and the banners and the newspapers everywhere.

It was the invasion of the Sudetenland that was the immediate cause of the refugee crisis in Prague in 1938. Germany had coveted these lands for a long time, and most of the inhabitants were ethnic German. Anyone who dreamed of a Greater Germany knew that it was a travesty that they were not the same colour on the maps as the Fatherland. Indeed, it was believed that since at one time they had been a part of Germany, their transferal to Czechoslovakia after World War I was a great historical injustice. At Munich Hitler's relentless pressure paid off, and England and France agreed to his takeover of the Sudetenland in return for Peace For Our Time. And so the German war machine moved in, and the refugee crisis began.

The refugees came largely from two groups. On the one hand there were those who had opposed, so long and so bitterly, the nazification of their region. They were Socialists or, even worse as far as Hitler was concerned, Communists, and they were the leaders of their various communities, not only politicians but also doctors, lawyers, artists and teachers. It is estimated that about 2000 of them were "marked men". Loathed by the Nazis for their opposition, they were fearful about their fate were they to be captured. They assumed that at best it would be a concentration camp and a drastically reduced life expectancy. And then there were the families of these men, the thousands of women and children who went with their menfolk, and also the even greater number of lesser party workers (and their families) who followed their leaders out of the occupied homelands.

And then there were the Jews, another of Hitler's favourite hate groups. After Kristallnacht few Jews could have had much optimism about the future – although surely none could have imagined how terrible that future was to become. But in 1938 it was the Socialists who were considered to be in the greater danger. They were, or thought that they were, the more immediate political threat; the Jews, though corrupters of the nation, were pests who would be swatted off the German map in the fullness of time. In the early days they were even helped to emigrate as a means of getting rid of them; later there were to be other solutions.

And so all of them, both Socialist and Jew (and many were both) came rushing into the centre of Czechoslovakia in their tens of thousands like terrified creatures before a forest fire. The number is usually put at around 200,000. This was a refugee crisis similar to what has become familiar in Africa today, and then as now the authorities had no idea how to handle such large numbers. They certainly didn't want them in the middle of Prague, so they were billeted with their pots and pans and bits of bedding and whatever else they'd managed to salvage from their homes, in a variety of crumbling castles, abandoned hostels, schools and camps, fifty to one hundred kilometers outside the capital. Here whole families subsisted as best they could on intermittent handouts and soup kitchens.

It is now some seventy years since these catastrophic events, and with the help of this clarifying distance it is possible for accurate scholarship to come into its own, and the Prague refugee story may be told devoid of such distorting mirrors as the crude hyperboles of the media, the shallow, imitative chatter of the blog or the emotional exaggerations of hagiography. Certainly we can promise that there will be no ill-considered comparisons to Schindlers, Pimpernels, or Pied Pipers.

A great number of people from many countries were involved in the rescue of the Prague refugees. This book will concentrate mainly on the English contribution, and more specifically on the work of the British Committee for Refugees from Czechoslovakia (BCRC), the body that spearheaded the British rescue efforts. In any account of the activities of this organization, five names consistently come to the fore. They are Doreen Warriner, Nicholas Winton, Trevor Chadwick, Bill Barazetti and Beatrice Wellington. All of them, along with many, many others had been drawn to the city by the plight of the refugees, a plight that had been well publicized in the world's press and through myriad church networks. All, like Auden, were appalled by the madness that was destroying whole cultures, and wanted to try to help in some way. Each of these people will be the subject of a chapter in which their contribution to the Prague refugee story will be described and evaluated. In the past, some of these contributions have been told, though not always with the greatest accuracy. Some have not been given sufficient credit for what they achieved; some have been credited with slightly more than the facts might warrant. One has been given huge credit for the deeds of others. I hope this book will help to set the record straight.

DOREEN WARRINER

Doreen Warriner couldn't have known Auden's "1st September 1939" when she flew into Prague's brand new Ruzyne airport on October 13, 1938 - it was published almost a year later in The New Republic - but when she came to read it she would have understood it with the utmost clarity. It was why she was here. And yet as she disembarked on this cold October day she must have had mixed emotions. She was supposed to have been heading for the West Indies with her Rockefeller Fellowship where she had intended to study economic conditions. It all seemed a long way from where she was now, driving into Prague with what looked like a chilly, chaotic and, quite possibly, dangerous winter in front of her.

This was a city she knew well and loved, but as she drove down from the airport through the northern suburbs she was apprehensive about what she was going to find. Outwardly, of course, nothing had changed, except that she noted that there seemed to be rather more soldiers straggling rather aimlessly about the streets. The ancient boulevard of Wenceslas Square, the museum, the opera, the restaurants and theatres, the beauty of the Old Town, were all there as before. Prague was still one of the loveliest capitals of Europe, but it was clear to Warriner and almost everyone else, except possibly Neville Chamberlain, the British Prime Minister, that the city, indeed the whole country, and probably the continent itself were teetering on the edge of a huge disaster.

(Doreen Warriner 1904-1972)

According to her *Dictionary of National Biography* entry, Warriner was born on March 16, 1904 in Warwickshire. Her parents were middle class country people. Her father was a land agent, an estate manager, later a landowner, but she appears to have inherited her strong social conscience from her maternal grandfather, a priest in a poor parish in Staffordshire who had left Ireland due to his Fenian activities. She went to Malvern Girls' College (though Malvern Girls' College does not list her on their website alongside other "famous alumna" such as Barbara Cartland and Thandy Newton) and then on to St Hugh's College, Oxford from which she graduated when she was 22 with a first in Philosophy, Politics and Economics. Needless to say, like all women who went to university in those days, she was highly motivated and hugely intelligent. She continued rapidly up the academic ladder - research scholar at the London School of Economics; research fellow at Somerville College, Oxford; Ph.D in 1931; and at 29 she became an assistant lecturer at University College, London. The year was 1933, the year that Hitler became Chancellor of Germany.

Once in Prague Warriner went straight to her hotel, the new Art Deco palace, the Alcron at 40 Stepanska St., just off Wenceslas Square. Unfortunately she had no time to enjoy the Jazz Age decor. She had to.. ..well that was her first problem. How on earth was one supposed to tackle such a Herculean task? Where did one begin? She had about £450 in her pocket donated by various well-wishers, and out there in the villages around Prague there were some 200,000 despairing and destitute people. She had a vague notion that she would be handing out blankets and bowls of soup to long lines of refugees, but it all seemed so inadequate. As she later wrote,"I had no idea at all of what to do, only a desperate wish to do something."

Obviously it was first of all important to find out "what was going on", so as soon as she'd deposited her luggage in her room she went round to see the Quakers who had a large aid organisation, but discovered that they hadn't started relief work yet. From here she went to meet Wenzel Jaksch the leader of the Sudeten Social Democrats at his flat at Hermannova St. She found a sad figure whose life had been turned upside down by the invasion of his homeland. He was under no illusion that Germany would soon force the Czech government to hand over Sudeten anti-Nazi leaders like himself, and he would probably be killed; on the other hand to abandon his friends and followers was out of the question. It didn't help that he was also on crutches due to a recent car accident.

Back at the Alcron Hotel that night she met a reporter from The News Chronicle, a left-centre paper (until it was bought by The Daily Mail and closed) that supported refugee causes. He described to her how, a few days before, he'd seen

> *trainloads of refugees from the Sudetenland [beingl sent back into the occupied territory driven into the trains at the point of the bayonet; but that thousands of refugees from the Sudetenland still remained in Czech territory. He thought there were about 200,000.*

Doreen Warriner had been in Prague for precisely half a day, but the crash course in refugee conditions had been sharp and dramatic.

The next day, October 14, she went to the nearby Steiner

Hotel to meet two stalwarts of the British Labour Party, David Grenfell and its abrasive but immensely practical and energetic International Secretary, William Gillies. For the next two days they, in effect, took her under their wing. Their first stop was the British Legation in the swanky Thun Palace where she met various officials and in particular Gibson, the Passport Control Officer, whose warnings about the deteriorating situation and the dangers to the Sudeten Social Democrats confirmed their own fears. They then met Siegfried Taub the Vice President of the Sudeten Social Democrats, a man of enormous integrity who Warriner was to get to know well over the next few weeks.

But now it was the time for Lists. Lists were of crucial importance to the refugee process. Everyone had to be on a List in order to apply for a Visa. Lists were official. Lists could be taken to government offices and approved by men with rubber stamps sitting behind desks. Lists were important when places were scarce. With luck your name could move up a List and you'd end up on a train or a plane. With your name on a List you had proof of your existence. Under Gillies' direction, Taub, Grenfell and Doreen Warriner got down to the task of making a List of those who should be removed from Prague as quickly as possible. The problem was that initially there were some 2000 names of those who might be termed Social Democrat "leaders", and therefore in danger, but there was no hope of getting 2000 visas out of the British government in one go. Gillies, whose energy and directness had helped him fight many difficult causes, said they should try for 250. Warriner thought that this was wildly optimistic, but after a long day round the kitchen table the 2000 had been whittled down to 250. With Taub's help the leadership of a whole community had been listed, its teachers, politicians, artists and doctors, and now an attempt was to be made to take them to another country. Gillies, decisive as ever, left for London with Grenfell the next day clutching the precious List. Secretly he hoped for 100 visas. Not enough, but it would be a start. Both he and Grenfell had been extremely impressed by Warriner's commitment and intelligence during these discussions and asked her to be their contact in Prague.

In London they immediately had a meeting with Lord Halifax, the Foreign Minister during which they presumably touched on Britain's post Munich obligations to the abandoned Sudetenlanders, and managed to get a promise of 250 visas. This was on the understanding that the Labour Party would be responsible for the usual financial guarantees for the emigrants. Gillies agreed with alacrity even though the Labour Party didn't actually have the money. Two days later Grenfell was back in Prague.

Warriner must have been amazed at the speed of events. Five days before she "didn't know what to do" let alone how to do it. Now she was in the middle of a focused, practical and apparently successful rescue scheme, though she probably didn't realize that the frenetic pace was only just beginning. As soon as Grenfell returned, 50 Sudetenlanders were alerted for a fast departure by train. This presumably would have entailed masses of telephone calls, telegrams, and the rushed marshalling of visas, identification papers and so on. No one seemed to have any clear idea of routes and timetables; lines had been closed, connections had been cut off and everything had become confused and unreliable, but Grenfell simply decided to "find a way". They couldn't go through Germany with such a dangerous cargo of Socialists and Communists, so it was a question of travelling a few hundred kilometres eastwards to Poland, somehow crossing the border and then finding a connection to Krakow and Warsaw. Late in the evening of October 22 the first group of men said goodbye to their wives at Masaryk station and the train pulled out into the night.

It took them 30 hours to travel the 300 kilometres to Poland. One (unconfirmed) story claims that Grenfell himself paid for the coal at the border crossing, plus vodka for the train drivers. Whatever the means the men were safe, and Grenfell phoned Warriner from Krakow and told her to bring 20 more men right away by the same route. Nervous and battling 'flu she set off on the 25th.

> It was a long journey, all night by slow train into the depths of Slovakia, then by a motor train, passing the ruins of Orava castle up over a pass in the mountains, to the tiny frontier post of Sucha Hora. Here we had to wait the whole day - in this poor Slovak village where they could give us only eggs at their inn. Snow lay on the Tatra; we sat in the sun and my flu was cured. At last, at night, another tiny train appeared on the Polish side; we walked over the frontier, where there was an endless customs examination of the masses of luggage, but no real trouble. We journeyed on by slow train to Nowy Targ where we had missed the connection to Krakow, where Grenfell was waiting to meet us. Frozen and tired, we drank vodka in the waiting room.... I went on and after four hours met Grenfell in Krakow. He pushed me onto the express for Warsaw, gave me a plane ticket back to Prague and said, "Go back and get some more"....I was back in Prague by midday on the 27th.

Back in Prague the pressure was unrelenting. Warriner had to keep tabs on all the men destined for these early transports, go through the time consuming business of arranging for transit visas from the Polish consul, getting forms filled in, and generally handling family problems for those who were leaving. It was soon clear that she couldn't do all this and accompany the trains. But many volunteers were ready to step into the breach. Tessa Rowntree, who was working for the Quakers, took two trains; Alec Dickson of *The News Chronicle* took two; John Ingman of the Workers' Travel Association was also a courier. The trains left one after another as quickly as the papers were ready and within two weeks almost all the 250 men who had been considered to be in danger were out of the country.

And it was about now that Warriner slowly understood that the job, far from being almost finished, had barely started. As she writes in her memoir, "The real nature of the refugee problem I had not realized at all." It's true that the 250 men who had been brilliantly and speedily spirited to safety were those who had been in the most immediate danger, but it had been rather overlooked that they all had families. Now there were hundreds of women and children who had been separated from their menfolk, and many of them were without any means of support. And out in the camps there were literally thousands more - men, women and children - who had nowhere to go.

Through the early part of November Warriner visited the camps, sometimes in the company of Jaksch. These camps, dotted in all parts of the compass around Prague, some of them a two and a half hour drive away, were depressing places. They were unheated, food was rationed, blankets were scarce, broken windows were standard, and if the walls were green it probably wasn't due to paint. She began to spend her sparse funds on some medical supplies, blankets, wool for knitting, a few books, all pathetically inadequate attempts to make life more bearable. She particularly remembered one occasion when Jaksch, standing on the worn steps of what had once been a grand castle staircase, his face faintly lit by the light of an oil lamp, spoke to his followers quietly about their sorrows and their hopes. He spoke of the freedoms they'd fought for and the possibility of creating some sort of commune in South America. The scene moved her immensely and she couldn't help comparing the resilience and dignity of these apparently defeated Social Democrats with the Socialists she had met in England and elsewhere.

The sort of socialism I had known in England had been intellectual and rather spiteful in tone: middle-aged Fabians at conferences in the Home Counties, earnest and arrogant young Marxists at University College. Left Book Club readers in Hampstead.

Warriner could be quite sharp-tongued on occasion.

At the end of November, Sir Walter Layton, a man of some influence in both Whitehall and on Fleet Street, came to see the extent of the refugee situation in Prague, and before he left asked Warriner to administer *The News Chronicle* fund of some £7000, and also to be the official representative of The British Committee for Refugees from Czechoslovakia (BCRC). This was a voluntary organization composed of the major aid groups, such as The Labour Party, The News Chronicle, and the Quakers, who had realized that their effectiveness would be greater if they worked together. In other words, Warriner, now backed by money and an energetic association of aid groups had suddenly become the most important single player in the rescue of the Prague refugees. In just five weeks she had gone from novice aid-worker to veteran.

As always, responsibility brought with it not only a bigger office but tougher problems, and almost immediately she was faced with two of the latter. One concerned children. Like the old lady who lived in a shoe, she was somehow accumulating so many children, some abandoned, some lost, some needing special care, some with parents in jail, that she didn't know what to do. A few she'd arranged to put into the Y.W.C.A. and into a convenient "home", but their numbers seemed to be increasing. This was an on-going worry that she told the BCRC in London needed a solution.

Another potentially much more alarming problem hit her on November 25 when, without warning, the Polish Consul told her that he wouldn't give her any more transit visas for Poland. This basically meant that all the train routes through to the north coast of Europe were blocked. For the next eleven days she argued with the consul, and tried to find out the reason for the new travel prohibition, but all she got was surliness and increasing incivility. She suspected that Germany was putting pressure on the Poles for political reasons, but when on December 6 the consul told her that she could have the visas as long as her clients used a Polish shipping line when they got to the port of Gdynia she immediately smelt a rat. The next day, having alerted the British embassy she flew to Warsaw, and got herself taken to the Polish foreign office - where, as she half suspected, they had no idea what she was talking about. No, there was no problem with visas; no, there were no new travel prohibitions; the rules were just as they'd always been. She flew back to Prague the next morning, and no doubt rather enjoyed marching into the Polish Consul's office and telling him about her trip to Warsaw. Initially he didn't believe her, but when confirmation and pressure came not only from the British Legation but also from Warsaw he gave her the 150 transit visas she needed, though he swore to the last that all the travellers would be turned back at the Polish border. To be on the safe side she went with this group of refugees, and saw them across the frontier at Ostrava - where the guards were as pleasant as they'd always been. Warriner's suspicion was that she'd almost fallen foul of a scam thought up by Cedok (then as now) the Czech travel agency and the Gdynia-America ship line, involving rake-offs in high places, plus other forms of skulduggery. Whether this was so or not will never now be known, but the whole experience was a sobering lesson in the fragility of the transports and how underhand "official" dealings could so easily cause disaster. On the brighter side, the episode perhaps taught Warriner herself some tricks that would stand her in good stead later when she indulged in a few underground railway manoeuvres of her own.

It was also at this time that she learnt something about the slippery world of public relations. As the days passed she had become more and more frustrated by the slowness with which the British visas were arriving. It seemed to her that the people in London simply didn't understand the squalor and misery in which the refugees lived and how many thousands there were who needed to be got out of the country, and that time was short. She was also a little irritated by the number of people who kept arriving on flying visits "to see how things were". No doubt some were a bit like the modern celebrity who hopes to add to his or her glitter by means of a day or two hugging poverty in Africa for a glossy magazine. For these sorts of reasons she wrote an extraordinarily blunt and heartfelt letter to the press. It appeared in *The Daily Telegraph* on December 12.

She begins by mentioning the camps which are "appallingly overcrowded", usually without heat, and she implies that some of the local authorities are probably pilfering the meagre food allowances. As for attempts to administer direct relief from the British Lord Mayor's Fund, this is being achieved "with the maximum inefficiency and delay". In a later sentence that drips with muted scorn she dismisses the ridiculous do-goodery of most donors: "In the last few days 1 have received several offers of cigarettes and chocolates for Christmas..... which indicates that there is some confusion in Great Britain about the real state of affairs". She then turns her anger on the middle classes who always get to the front of the queue because they have money and sharp elbows and know how to work the system, whereas the poor, who throughout her life were Warriner's main concern, were left behind. Her conclusion is uncompromising. All those donations of chocolates and cigarettes and the odd fiver slipped into the collection plate are no better "than a palliative for one's own conscience".

These were strong words indeed, and one can see why the officials of various home charities were somewhat apoplectic. And it is probably true that such a letter would not improve charitable donations. Culpin, the chairman of the BCRC, fired off a crisp, two line telegram to her: "Letter in *Daily Telegraph* has made great trouble. You must refrain from such pronouncements." And, as she was to be in London in a few days, "I'll see you in my study shortly" also hung in the air.

On December 21 she flew to London mainly to plead with

the authorities for a faster delivery of more visas, but first she had to face the anger her letter had aroused. The Chairman of the BCRC gave her a stern lecture, and told her that her intemperance had probably lost them £100,000, presumably because she'd offended all those well-meaning people from the home counties who thought refugee aid was mainly a matter of woolly gloves and tins of spam. The head of the Lord Mayor's Fund wanted her sacked immediately, but with strong supporters like Gillies on the committee his demand was ignored. She herself wasn't much concerned. She'd made her point and she hadn't come to London to squabble. Besides she had to get back to Prague to get another transport organized. But when she left the next day she had no extra visas in her pocket.

That Christmas was a low point for Warriner. She had been held up in Paris by fog, and only arrived back on Christmas Eve.

> *Snow was falling heavily and a bitter cold had set in. I had stupidly believed I could bring back some hope for the camps, but there was none. On Christmas morning I went round to see the children in the YWCA and the home, with presents, and there heard of the diptheria epidemic [in one of the camps] in which four children died....I went for a walk in the snow in the hills, and came back in the evening into the lighted town. Prague in the snow is so beautiful that I could forget the horrors for a time, and my mind felt steadier.*

It was at this Christmas season that the four other players of the Prague refugee story make their appearance. Nicholas Winton, a London stockbroker, who was heading for a skiing holiday, was summoned to the city by his friend, Martin Blake. He very quickly evaluated the awful situation, particularly as it impacted on children, and resolved under Warriner's tutelage to start the Kindertransports. He stayed in Prague for three weeks. Trevor Chadwick, a schoolmaster, came to Prague to find two children to take back to the family school in Swanage. He met up with Winton and helped him set up the Kindertransports. There is no record that he met Warriner at this time but as she was at the hub of all refugee affairs he must have done so. There is ample evidence that they later worked very closely together. Bill Barazetti remains something of a mystery. He and his family were refugees, and he began to make himself useful to Warriner and became a jack of all trades in her office. Winton met him there at the beginning of January and refers to him as her "secretary". His later history is, as we shall see, extremely murky. Finally, the remarkable Beatrice Wellington wafted in from the Canadian West. She was a law unto herself, and lesser mortals such as those in the BCRC, or the British government or the Gestapo were no match for such a force of nature.

All four are fascinating characters, and we will look at each one in turn to find out what their contributions were to the rescue of the thousands of Prague refugees and, equally interestingly, how posterity has evaluated and rewarded these contributions.

Though Christmas 1938 was bleak for Doreen Warrener, by Twelfth Night it was clear that there was going to be a significant change in the refugees' fortunes. A loan that had been under negotiation for some time was finally agreed. Motivated by genuine humanitarian concerns, and no doubt also prodded by post-Munich guilt, Britain and France were offering a 12 million pound loan to the Czech government, of which 4 million was to be a free gift for emigration. Several thousand Sudeten families would be given £200 each (the equivalent today of about £5000) to start a new life in a new country. As Stopford, the new British Liaison Officer for Refugees at the Prague Legation later wrote, "It was this provision of official financial assistance which made the whole scheme so important in the history of refugee movements". The sea change was in the new perception that the outside world now had of these refugees. No longer were they a long line of the poor and the dispossessed in ragged clothes extending begging bowls outside government offices. Now they had the means to support themselves, and they could contribute to the well being of their chosen country.

The knock-on effect was immediate, particularly in Canada. With the help of a sympathetic government and railway companies that controlled emigration, more than 1000 Sudetens headed for Canada, some to Saskatchewan and some to the Peace River District in British Columbia. Warriner wryly observes that "it was not Labour-governed Australia or New Zealand which opened the doors [to the refugees], but capitalist Canada. In the countries where government controlled immigration, every initiative was rejected; the trade unions set themselves rigidly against it." Walter Schoen tells the story of the Canadian settlement in *The Tupper Boys*, where he describes the culture shock of suddenly exchanging the old, civilized urban life of the Sudeten for the wild open spaces, frigid temperatures, log cabin construction, shooting moose, trapping beaver, and learning how to avoid grizzly bears and black flies. Life, as he says, was hard for a long time but, as they often reminded themselves, the hardships didn't include the Gestapo.

Here we must stop for a moment to mention a sixth

participant in the Prague rescues. If one were to ask any former refugees whether they had ever heard the name R.J. Stopford almost certainly one would get a blank look, but the claim can fairly be made that in fact he facilitated the exit of more refugees than the other five put together. "Bobbie" Stopford was a civil servant, the quintessential government official. He was appointed to administer the Free Gift Fund and as British Liaison Minister for Refugees he worked with the aid groups, the Czech government, and later the Germans. As we would say today, he was a safe pair of hands. Like so many in the world of diplomacy, he was never a figurehead himself but without him and his like, delicate negotiations would falter. In group photos of great political occasions he would be one of those peering over the shoulder of the front row speaker, his face slightly out of focus. Later in life he was awarded a C.M.G. Rather than have a chapter of his own, he will feature prominently in the stories of the other five.

As Mr Moneybags and also as a British Government official, Stopford was as important to the refugee effort as Doreen Warriner. In fact the two became the perfect team, especially after the Gestapo arrived. Stopford, the highly respected diplomat with embassy status, who could talk to all the players at the highest level; and Warriner a more impulsive figure, unconstrained by protocol, who worked in the field but needed guidance and advice when her operations became somewhat illegal. The two remained firm friends after the war.

But even though the funds had become available with the Free Gift, there was absolutely no guarantee that the refugee camps would be cleared before whatever was going to happen, happened. It was a sort of blind race against time where no one knew when it would end or where the finishing post was.

All that was certain was that the bureaucracies in London were elephantine, the Home Office devoid of urgency, and the Wehrmacht getting ever nearer and noisier.

On January 14 the formidable Eleanor Rathbone, Independent member of parliament for the Combined Universities, visited Prague on a fact finding mission. She was a force to be reckoned with at Westminster and fought for her favourite causes (women's rights, fair treatment for Czechoslovakia, and indeed injustice of any sort) with such vigour that it was said that junior ministers hid behind pillars when they saw her coming down the corridor. But Warriner was delighted to see her because unlike so many others in England she had persuasive powers and she was under no illusions about Hitler's intentions. However she sensed that even this redoubtable lady couldn't see the imminence of the threat, and the desperate problems that she faced - too many refugees, too few visas, a shortage of transport and only about six weeks before the jack boots were on the streets of Prague. (In fact she was wrong about the six weeks; the German army would march into Prague in eight weeks). Rathbone thought that poor Warriner was getting a bit stressed out due to her workload, and advised her to relax, but she promised to work on her parliamentary colleagues to try and speed up the visa situation.

So through January the visas continued to dribble in at an agonizingly slow rate, maybe 30 or 40 a week, and small inroads were made into the numbers in the wretched camps. But her patience finally reached breaking point on the night of January 27th. She'd just returned to the Alcron after a long day of meetings and form filling and interviews, and went to the bar for her usual stiff tomato juice. Just leaving were a group of extremely jovial Germans who were giving each other the 1939 equivalent of Teutonic high fives. When the little Jewish bartender brought her her drink his hands were shaking and the redness of his hair was emphasized by the whiteness of his face. She asked him why the Germans had been so happy, and he whispered, "They say Czechoslovakia's going to be next. Soon." "When?" "The middle of March."

The next day she collected the names of the six hundred families still in the camps and booked a flight to London. It was time to pester the Home Office again. She managed to arrange an immediate BCRC meeting where she waved her list of 600 families and spoke about the danger, but initially the response was unpromising. The discussion got bogged down in talk about who was in most danger, and which names should be prioritized, and whether families could stay in Czechoslovakia until their men were settled elsewhere, and so on. It was as though the geographical distance from the problem anaesthetized any ability to grapple with it. As Warriner was later to write, "In Prague we lived on tenterhooks, but London was detached and calm: it was impossible to get through the cotton wool which prevented them from hearing". But she was wrong. Also on the committee was her old friend William Gillies who, ever the man of action, took her list of 600, without consulting the BCRC, straight to the Home Office - who approved it. Furthermore, she herself went to the Home Office and managed to work out a new method of speeding up the visas. No longer would there be the immensely time consuming requirements of form filling. (Name? Where did you live? What's your occupation? Age? Family? Are you now or have you ever been.....? Right! Now we're going to check all this and we'll see you in a few days")

Instead the entire group were to be issued with purple cards. Essentially all that would be required would be Warriner's approval, then the passport could get a purple card and it could then be stamped. It was also agreed that the Poles might be leaned on a little bit to see whether they could issue their transit visas with more dispatch.

In February there was much more hope in the air. Even the sun was shining as her plane came in to land at Ruzyne on February 2. With the new emigration system she could get many more people away, and there was even a chance that the camps would be cleared in time. At this time she worked next to Siegfried Taub, the Vice President of the Sudeten Social Democrats, who continued to impress her with his loyalty and decency, and with two local volunteers, Hilde Patz and Alois Mollik "the best workers I have ever known". They worked fourteen hour days as the visa lists came through with increasing speed, organizing train transports, wrestling with timetables, sending telegrams to camps making constant trips to consulates, especially the Poles who liked to create problems, and interviewing refugees with their thousands of travel problems. In the middle of February she got a transport off with 500 aboard, half to England and half to Sweden, and two of the camps were emptied.

But even while Warriner was experiencing a certain euphoria, the scholar in her was conscious of the wider implications and future effects of her small victories:

> *For us in Prague, it meant relief and hope. But for Europe it meant that the last defenders of German liberty were leaving, five hundred German Socialists who might never see their home again, whom Europe could not tolerate. The emigration of the Sudetens meant the departure of the*

elite of the working class from the advanced industrial area of Central Europe. Highly skilled men with high standards of living in the finest sense....The great emigrations have usually been made by those who opposed oppression: we were in the tradition.

At the beginning of March the streets and cafés and bars of Prague were filled with whisper, buzz and false report about the German invasion. Some said the German army was on its way; others that it was nowhere to be seen. Some had talked to someone else who knew a man who was almost certain that a friend had seen Czech troops moving to the frontier, though whether this was to help or hinder the enemy was a matter of debate. Everyone knew what Hitler was up to, but when he was going to get up to whatever it was to which he was clearly up was another matter. Some shook their heads and said it would all blow over; others knew it was the day after tomorrow and laid in extra stores; Jaksch who was in great personal danger, was confident that he was safe until the end of the month. But Jaksch was wrong. Through it all the refugee rescue operations went steadily on, and the camps slowly emptied. The lucky 20 children on Chadwick's first air transport had packed their teddy bears ready for departure on the 12th but this was changed at the last minute to Tuesday, 14th.

On March 13th Warriner went down to the British Legation as usual and found the rumours there were swirling as vigorously as anywhere. At this point she still had several hundred women and children in the camps. Gibson, the Passport Control Officer, had a long face and was shaking his head. Stopford took her aside and warned her that she might not be able to get her people out, but he would cable London that the situation was desperate. Late that night she phoned Gillies who, ever the man of action, told her, "Get the women in from the camps! All of them! Send telegrams tomorrow to all the camps, and tell them to be at Wilson station by tomorrow evening! Can you have a train standing by?" "Yes. But some of the camps are many hours away. I could make it for the day after tomorrow". "No! Tomorrow! Tell them to move fast!"

Meanwhile Gibson had agreed that if he got clearance in principle from London he'd give a group visa to anyone on her list. The next day, March 14, the women and children and a few men from the nearer camps began to arrive at the station. And the official news also came in that the German army was on the move and had already occupied the towns on the Polish border. By 6 p.m. there were 500 refugees sitting in the train as it waited in the station, while Warriner, as nervous as Bluebeard's wife, paced the platform and prayed that the visas would arrive in time. At 7p.m. she was told that the clearance had come through from London and she dashed back to the Legation, had the Lists checked and was back at the station by 9 p.m.. The train pulled out at 11 p.m., without any guarantee that it was actually going to get through to Poland. There were still only 500 women and children on board, leaving 200 unaccounted for. The story goes that when the train reached Ostrava, the border town, in the early hours of Wednesday morning, they found it full of German troops. But Ingman, the courier, had ordered all the blinds to be pulled down and when the train slowed he shouted to the Germans, "You'll never guess what I've got in here. A load of dirty Jews!" and he was waved through with much laughter. It is impossible to vouch for the accuracy of the tale.

For Warriner, Wednesday, March 15, was a blur. The phone calls from London started coming in early in the morning with information from BBC bulletins that German soldiers were crossing the frontier, but by noon she didn't need the news flashes. They'd arrived in the city and she was rubbing shoulders with the German High Command in the public spaces of the Alcron Hotel. Making an urgent phone call in the lobby was made slightly trickier by the presence of noisy Oberstleutnants beside her phoning their wives. Several times that day she made the circuit between the hotel, the BCRC offices and the British Legation. At each of these places she was besieged by desperate refugees making what they thought were last desperate efforts to get out. Luckily she'd cleared the bank of all her aid funds and had about £5000 on her, so if they were on her lists she pressed money into their hands, scribbled a note on her calling card and told them to get out any way they could, by train, by car, by bus, by bicycle if necessary, and make their way to the British consulate in Katowice in southern Poland, and show them the note. It was the best she could do. As well as all this, she had to collect up the many passports she had in her office and destroy a lot of papers and documents that might be incriminating if they fell into the wrong hands - the names of her refugees, their associates, their past histories, the anti Nazi comments. By now the afternoon was becoming dark, and the snow that had started earlier was falling heavily. On one taxi trip to the Legation with her boxes of documents she found herself a part of a German army convoy that was inching along in the deepening snow. At the Charles bridge everything stopped to let a line of infantry march across:

I got out not wishing to stop there and watch, and went into the Krizovnicka church by the bridgehead. It was completely full, and absolutely silent; no mass was being said, but everyone was kneeling. I waited for a time and then went back to the taxi.

Amidst the panic, the trauma, the soldiers and the snow there were still amusing vignettes. Stopford, remembered driving with Troutbeck of the British Legation up a steep hill behind the Legation where the wheels of their car began to spin just as they passed a troop of soldiers:

As I got out to push, Troutbeck said, "Don't let those damn Germans touch my car. I will not be helped by them". At that moment the leading troops broke ranks and joined me in pushing behind the car, while Troutbeck, all unconscious of what was happening, congratulated me on my strength.

Later, Stopford was at the Charles Bridge where Warriner had stopped earlier. On either side of the bridge were narrow footways that

had long been treated as one way streets by pedestrians. Some stray German soldiers, ignorant of this rule, started to cross on the wrong side, only to be met by an indignant old woman who went for them with her umbrella and drove them back in disorder.

He goes on,

But on the whole, the Army drove in like a Victory Parade, while the Czechs looked on sullenly, sadly realizing that their few years of freedom were over and that they were once more under the Teutonic oppression which they had endured for centuries before 1918.

That morning, before the German Army actually entered the city, the British Legation offered asylum to certain members of the foreign press who thought they might have been too heavy-handed in their anti-Nazi comments, and also to "a small number of people who were in great danger and who had some special claim on us". Stopford divides them into three categories; (i) officials of the Sudeten Social Democratic Party, including Jaksch and Taub and his family; (ii) a communist called Katz; (iii) "Herr Barazetti, a member of Miss Warriner's Secretariat." Stopford gives no reason for the latter's inclusion. Apparently at the time he only had a Czech interim passport, though why this was so and whether it made a difference to his safety is unclear. It is curious that Warriner, who also writes about this incident doesn't mention that her erstwhile "secretary" was a member of the group. We will come to Barazetti's strange biography later. Certainly she would have been greatly saddened by the departure of the two Sudeten leaders though she knew they had to save themselves. They were men with whom she had worked closely for four months, and for whom she had developed tremendous respect.

But her work, which had been exhausting and difficult enough up to this point, was about to become a great deal harder. The day after the invasion she was working in her temporary office in the Legation when two women pushed through the crowd of refugees. They were two of the "lost ones" who had been summoned three days earlier, but their camp was one of the furthest away, and now they'd at last managed to get to the Masaryk railway station. And, oh yes, there were thirty more women waiting at the station. And they had their children with them. About fifty of them. Warriner set off immediately with her two helpers, Margaret Dougan and Christine Maxwell. The group they found at the station was a sorry sight, having been on the road for more than two days with little sleep and less food. Having got them a bite to eat, the next problem was finding them somewhere to stay while transport was arranged. This was easier said than done as all the hotels, even the cheapest ones, had been requisitioned by the German military. Warriner decided that their best chance lay in the suburbs, and told Dougan to go as quickly as possible to Chuchle just over the Vlatava River and see what she could find, and she'd follow with everyone else as quickly as possible. Their progress was tortuous. She tried to break them up into smaller groups in order to remain reasonably inconspicuous, but she herself had to rush backwards and forwards in order to keep everyone in touch. The whole situation was made even more nightmarish by the parade in honour of the Fuehrer who had come to Prague to celebrate his famous victory. They kept on being forced to take detours because the streets, which were crawling with soldiers, were blocked off. And then there were the children, so many of whom had to be carried or urged constantly to "keep up". One of the mothers fainted, so she was put into a taxi with Maxwell and sent on ahead. The rest had to stop and get something to eat at a restaurant. Then they went on, but when they suddenly came on a taxi rank, Warriner decided they'd all had enough and hired the whole lot to take them to Chuchle where, "to my great relief Margaret Dougan had found three small hotels with enough room to take them all. The women cried and kissed me, delighted to see real white beds again, though to me they seemed very small and hard".

By this time she was feeling that she could do with a lie down in her own bed, and it was then that someone told her that she was almost certain that there was another group of women and children at Wilson Station, the other railway station in the centre of Prague.

> *So back I went and found there another group of about thirty women with their children, still more exhausted and still hungrier. I fed them at the station and again looked for rooms, this time in the slum quarter of Zizkiv. At last I found a small shabby hotel, with seven dark rooms in the attics; the lower floors were occupied by German soldiers. The Czech proprietor was doubtful when I told him who the women were, but then said "They are your friends; if they will keep quiet they can have the rooms." Money helped, of course; I paid a week in advance.*

The women on her lists slowly drifted in and the camps emptied, but at the end of March she was still responsible for nearly 250 women and children, plus a few men who had entered her orbit, and all of them were now living in a half a dozen grubby little hotels in Prague and its suburbs. To begin with life was relatively straightforward. An army of occupation has more important things to worry about than refugees who, as long as they stay out of the way, probably won't get into trouble. But of course as the days passed the more sinister uniform of the Gestapo began to appear with more frequency, and more oppressive rules and regulations were put in place. It was as though a more efficient security noose was being placed around the refugees and slowly tightened.

Tougher regulations were coming into force. The Gestapo

added another requirement to the already existing need for passports and transit visas and entry visas that refugees needed. From now on they would also require an exit visa. These could only be obtained courtesy of the Gestapo. In the early days they were given out quite freely, especially to the Jewish children, in whom the authorities had little interest; later, getting an exit visa was less easy and more dangerous. At the end of March Warriner had a brutal introduction to what lay ahead. On March 30, she discovered that three of her women had been refused exit visas because they or their husbands had connections to communist organizations, and that night she learnt that one of her hotels had been discovered by the Gestapo, and two men and a woman had been taken away for questioning.

She had passports for some of her refugees, mainly the Communists, which was fortunate as they were in most danger of being arrested. Other passports had been lost, or stolen or confiscated. It appears that the Gestapo had seized some when they raided her office. Clearly, the authorities were actively interfering with the movements of the refugee. On March 31 Warriner had arranged for another group to leave. That afternoon she packed sandwiches for seventy with Trevor Chadwick who was himself getting ready for his second Kindertransport. Down at Wilson station they found everything quiet, perhaps too quiet. No police, no railway staff except for a ticket collector on the gate to the platform. The train was about to leave so the two decided to go, but when they got to the platform gate the official shut it and wouldn't let them leave. Suddenly a gang of what can only be described as thugs rushed past them and down onto the platform. Chadwick and Warriner followed. The men, who were in plain clothes, were running up and down the train, banging on the windows and shouting loudly. They hustled two people roughly off the train, a man, and a woman called Wanda Bauernfeind. Warriner went up to the gang leader asked what they were doing, and got insults for her pains. She asked what they wanted with Wanda. "This woman has a visa for England, and she has an exit permit signed by the Gestapo. Why can't she leave?" "The Gestapo don't give reasons", was the reply. "Especially not to people who deal in communist [dreck] muck. They're no better than muck themselves." And the hammering and the yelling at the shunting of the train and the smashing of lavatory doors went on until they all marched off. It was Warriner the analytical academic who described the psychology of what she'd just witnessed:

> *On that night at the Wilson station their technique was displayed. There is no question of justice or mercy....they came to terrorize, to reduce everyone to a state of helplessness and fear. There is no system, only a boiling cauldron into which every now and again a certain quantity of bones and blood must be thrown; it doesn't matter whose, but it does matter that those who are still free should see and tremble. All the dramatic effects were deliberate - the searching glare at my passport, the shunting of the train and so on. It gets on one's nerves and is meant to do. Because behind all the theatricality there is the reality: the concentration camps are filling, people do not return. Nothing has been heard of Wanda Bauernfeind since last night.*

Warriner, of course, still had many women and children hidden away in her hotels and because it was inevitable that eventually the Gestapo would discover them all, Stopford, as an official of His Majesty's Government, undertook to try and negotiate for those whose passports were held by the police and to try and get them their exit visas. Being a diplomat of some standing he was in a position to talk to people high up in the Foreign Ministry and the Gestapo. He made an appointment to see Herr Kriminalrat von Boemelberg the number two man in the Gestapo at their headquarters in the Petschek Bank Building. He describes the meeting in his memoir, *Prague 1938/39*:

> *Having asked for him at the enquiry office, I was in turn asked by an Ordner in uniform, what his room number was and told that, if I did not know it, I could not see him. Irritated, I said I had an appointment with him and if I was not immediately taken to him, I would return to the Legation and telegraph London to say that I was being impeded by the Gestapo in carrying out an agreement made between the British and German governments. I was at once taken upstairs and shown into a room where a man was writing at a desk, who, without looking up, asked who I was. When I replied, he asked if I was "Herr Stopford himself" and then welcomed me warmly and apologized, saying that he had been told that I was sending a representative to see him.*

The two men then discussed the passport situation, and it was agreed that the women could have them back as long as Boemelberg could meet them and try to persuade them not to leave as they were perfectly safe in the arms of the Fatherland. He met them the next day, persuaded none of them to stay and didn't give them back their passports.

> *When I called him and asked him why he had not done so, he said that only half of them had passports and what were we going to do about the others? I said that he must*

> *issue some sort of travel documents with exit permits to the others, and that this last minute delay was monstrous, as I must put off the train till next day, by which time he must have the papers ready. He replied that the next day was the Fuehrer' birthday when nobody was allowed to work. I said that I did not care whose birthday it was, that I was prepared to work and that if I could, surely he could too. During all this I was banging the table, holding the telephone close to it so as I could be sure he could hear me.*

About half the women left two days later, and the last of them left after two months.

> *At one of our meetings the Kriminalrat told me that the reason for the hold-up was that he had discovered that some "dirty Jews" had been forging pussports. What he did not tell me was that it was some of his own staff who had – for a consideration – been forging the passports.*

The matter of forged passports is an interesting one. It is unclear who was responsible for the traffic in illegal exit documents in Prague in 1939 and indeed for the ways in which many escaped the country, but it is certain that a large number left without the approval of the Gestapo. Almost all the main players in this story claimed credit for the bribery and corruption at one stage or another, and it certainly seems to have been endemic to the whole refugee operation.

Beatrice Wellington seemed to have a happy knack of coming up with blank passports for those whose applications had been turned down, though she doesn't say where she obtained these blank forms. Chadwick, in his account of his experiences in Karen Gershon's *We Came As Children* wrote,

I had my guarantors lined up and the children waiting. The next transport was taking shape. There had to be documents, so I had some made, as near as possible like the Home Office ones, and away the train went. I informed everybody and awaited the Home Office telegram in reply. I betted myself that it would contain the word "irregular" and I won.

Barazetti, of course, in the largely inaccurate biography printed in his Times Obituary (October 2000) claimed that "because the English visas were often slow to come through I got a Jewish printer in Prague to produce forged papers to show to the German authorities." (One notes how very close this is to Chadwick's forgery statement!) But it seems fairly clear that it was Doreen Warriner herself who was at the centre of the illegal movement of refugees, and the associated fake documentation and that Stopford knew all about it. Indeed, she made life a little awkward for Stopford who as a British diplomat could not possibly be seen to be involved in such illegalities. As he says,

Miss Warriner and l had agreed that I, as an official representative of the British Government, must confine myself to negotiations about legal emigration, as any connection with illegal emigration would have ruined my official work. But we.....turned a blind eye on her connection with the elaborate organization which helped refugees escape who were in great danger and obviously would not get official permission to leave. If I came across such cases, l used to tell her of them and leave it at that. It was an unfair division of risk, but one which could not be avoided.

Warriner's ingenuity when it came to cutting corners when the safety of her refugees was threatened seems to have become legendary. *The Oxford Dictionary of National Biography* tells us that "a brilliant improvisor, she would bribe a consul with rare postage stamps, or a train conductor to keep her compartment door locked, or steal a general's visiting card that might come in handy." The bribing of the Polish consul with her stamp collection sounds a bit far-fetched, and may have metamorphosed from bribery for visa "stamps", but the fact remains that she ran an extensive underground railway system for those in real danger.

It was inevitable, of course, that the whole illegal operation would be discovered, the only unknown being whether this would be sooner or later. For Warriner it was sooner. The Gestapo were becoming increasingly angry about the number of "wanted men" who were slipping through their fingers, and they were becoming more efficient as the weeks passed. On April 14, at 6 am. they burst into the hostel where Christine Maxwell and Margaret Dougan, Warriner's two main assistants, had their rooms. Neither were there, (they were probably guiding an illegal train to Poland) so they went next door and took Beatrice Wellington in for questioning instead. When Maxwell and Dougan returned, Stopford told them that the Gestapo obviously knew of their illegal escapades and that rather than compromise the legitimate transports they should leave Prague. He put them on a train the next day. Meanwhile he had also promised von Boemelberg that "if he ever produced to me real evidence that any English person was engaged in [illegal] work I would see that he or she left the country at once". On April 22 Boemelberg showed him his file on Warriner in which there was one of her calling cards on which was written in her highly distinctive, though nearly illegible, hand a note of introduction of a refugee to the

Englishman in charge of the escape route across the Polish frontier. Warriner, in danger of arrest, had to leave immediately.

April 23, her last day in Prague, was a sad one. She went round to all the hotels to say goodbye to her women. "About 120 were left. It was misery to have to tell them I was leaving, though they knew why; they could not believe that they were certain to get out, as I believed they were. So many heroines." Next she arranged for Chadwick to look after "some children who were left alone, because their mothers had been arrested", and checked that the eighty or so women and children eligible for the final transport were ready.

> *Podhajsky came to say goodbye, and drove me up the Petrin hill to see Prague for the last time. Since I had first visited it ten years ago, I had got to know it well, this winter better than ever. I wondered if l would ever see it again. But Podhajsky was sure that the occupation would not last more than a few months.*

Down at the station the Gestapo were making their usual belligerent presence felt, but the train left for the Polish border without incident at 11 p.m.. The Gestapo came to arrest Warriner five days later.

* * *

After Doreen Warriner left there were four and a half months before war was declared. The gradual drift towards hostilities was evident for both the refugees and for those who were trying to help them. The British Legation was withdrawn on May 25. The BCRC was coming to an end as a voluntary organisation because it didn't receive the donations needed for the increasing number of refugees trying to escape, and it metamorphosed in July into a semi-governmental body called the Czech Refugee Trust Fund (CRTF). The new representative in Prague, Walter Creighton, was a government man and not at all interested in clandestine operations. But the real power behind the emigration changes of June, July and August was the Gestapo. They had finally got tired of the buccaneering tendencies of the BCRC volunteers and their ad hoc methods, and were determined to put a stop to them. Soon after the German army invaded Stopford had already warned London that most of the BCRC people would have to be replaced by those who weren't compromised by all sorts of illegal dealings. By May 9th Stopford had been "told by the Gestapo that they knew all about the British Committee's representatives' connections with the underground railway and that all their work in Prague would have to cease immediately if they did not stop helping illegal emigration."

All the former BCRC auxiliaries were sent home with the splendid exception of Beatrice Wellington, the Canadian, who refused to take orders from anybody, and that included the British Government and the Gestapo.

But it was the Gestapo who were now in control and they rather cleverly exercised it through the Refugee Institute, a Jewish emigration organization in Prague. In effect they pretended to empower the Institute with full control over emigration. Only the Institute could issue exit visas, and on June 22 the Institute wrote to Creighton to say that now the official arrangement with the Germans was that all refugee work was to be concentrated in the Institute. The Gestapo were all sweetness and light. In July they happily announced the creation, in Stopford's words, *of a Central Office to deal with the emigration of Jews, in which Czechs and Germans would work together. The German authorities wished to put at the disposal of this office the experience they had gained in emigration work, especially with regard to the appropriation of currency and the provision of possibilities of emigration. There would be another meeting in a few days time at Gestapo headquarters.*

Thus did the Gestapo lull the Institute into co-operation. The words of Grey's "Elegy" would seem to be appropriate:

> *Alas, regardless of their doom*
> *The little victims play!*
> *No sense have they of ills to come,*
> *Nor care beyond today.*

One wonders whether the leaders of the Institute realized that all these policies on behalf of Prague Jewry were being orchestrated from Vienna where there was a new Gestapo chief. His name was Adolf Eichmann. At the time, of course, no one knew of the terrible talents of this man. And why indeed should anyone be suspicious? The Jews had been encouraged to emigrate; the Gestapo had little interest in them. The more that left the merrier. It was the Socialists and Communists they hated. It was only later that these matters changed.

After returning to England Doreen Warriner worked at the Ministry of Economic Warfare in London and then at the Political Warfare Executive. In 1943 she went to the Middle East and later to Yugoslavia where she continued to do relief work. Eventually she returned to her academic life at the University of London where she became a professor in the

School of Slavonic and East European Studies, and where, in her books and scholarly articles, she argued for the poor and the dispossessed just as she had fought for the disadvantaged in Prague many years earlier. She died of a stroke on December 17, 1972 at the relatively young age of 68.

Of her work in Prague in 1938/39 the DNB says, "She held the whole disparate volunteer rescue enterprise together by sheer force of personality." It is impossible to say how many people she was directly responsible for saving, but it certainly ran into the thousands. In other words, for purposes of comparisons some five or six times the number that were rescued on the famous Prague Kindertransports. She received an OBE for this work in 1941.

The last words belong to her old friend Stopford in a letter to The Times written shortly after her obituary appeared. A draft is in the Stopford papers at the Imperial War Museum:

> *When I arrived in Prague in November.....I found her in charge of a small band of devoted women sent out by the British Committee for Refugees from Czechoslovakia. We worked in close co-operation, she dealing with the individual refugees.....and I with the governments concerned. She also organized the escape of refugees especially wanted by the Gestapo through the illegal underground railway into Poland, until the Gestapo obtained evidence against her on this count and I persuaded her to leave the country, for fear that she would unwittingly lead the Gestapo to refugees on their wanted list. In fact the Gestapo were considering her arrest.*
> *Altogether over 15,000 refugees were enabled to emigrate by the British Fund, a great number of whom owed their lives to her unremitting devotion to their cause and to the energy with which she worked on their behalf, regardless of the risks she herself ran.*

NICHOLAS WINTON

Nicholas Winton's entry in *Who's Who* is typically modest. If length is any indication of worth then in comparison with those he shares a page with he has less to say for himself than Jeanette Winterson, and about the same as Norman Wisdom. One notes perhaps the whiff of achievement in the opening fact (" Kt 2003") but there is nothing else to mark him out from the great and the good except for the curious citation towards the end, "Order of Tomas Masaryk (Czech Republic)" and you have to go to Google to discover that this was awarded for "outstanding contributions to humanity, democracy and human rights". But you may still have to wonder what that was all about.

Winton's early life was unexceptional. His family, of German-Jewish origin, were well-to-do and lived in Hampstead. No doubt on Sunday afternoons they walked on the Heath, maybe over to Kenwood House when he was twelve to have a look at this recent gift to the nation. He went to a brand new public school, Stowe, where he was happy and unhappy by fits and starts like everyone else. He wasn't particularly good at games which, in the strange culture of the public school, meant that he wasn't particularly popular. But then neither was he particularly unpopular. He did, however, take up the slightly aristocratic sport of fencing which he continued into his twenties and at which he very nearly represented Britain at the Olympics. Neither was he academically inclined, and therefore at eighteen he chose London and the world of banking rather than another three years of study at a university.

Nicholas Winton (1909 -)
With Hansi Neumann. Taken at Ruzyne Airport on January
12, 1939 just before the K.L.M. plane took off for Reading. This
was a Barbican Mission rescue flight. See also page 44)

His life in London was normal. He worked from 9 to 6, and in his spare time he went to parties and dances and the opera and Shakespeare. Although banking doesn't appear to have been a particularly gripping profession, he stuck with it and the day after his twentieth birthday went to Germany where he remained for three years to continue what was in effect an apprenticeship in international banking. He returned to London in 1931 and became a member of the Stock Exchange.

Up until then Winton had shown no particular signs of a social conscience or political leanings or religious persuasion. He had no interest in Judaism, and though, like many a schoolboy, he dabbled in Christianity at Stowe it was a passing interest. As far as we know he didn't deliver leaflets at election time, or do hospital volunteer work or join the boy scouts. Mencap and Abbeyfield were in the future. But in the second half of the 1930's events were occurring both personally and in the world at large that must certainly have disturbed the sequestered tenor of his way. The Spanish Civil War was in 1937; Munich was 1938; two months later there was Kristallnacht and the refugee crisis in the Sudetenland. Closer to home he could hardly help noticing the number of rather ragged, miserable Jewish relatives who came to visit his parents at their London house, and perhaps most important of all he made friends with a passionately left-wing master at Westminster school called Martin Blake. Gissing suggests that for Winton it was a relatively "sudden political maturity". Through Blake he got to know leading Labour Party figures such as Stafford Cripps, Tom Driberg, the charismatic Aneurin Bevan and his dynamic wife Jenny Lee. All of these influences and no doubt many more of a less obvious nature, were the preparation for his reaction when, in the midst of preparations for a two week skiing holiday in the Alps, he received the by now famous phone call from Blake that he must come to Prague instead because he had something to show him. Winton obediently put his skis back in the cupboard. Like Warriner and her Caribbean tour two months earlier, the holiday had to wait.

In Prague he immediately set about meeting the most important players in the refugee rescue efforts, visited the main aid organizations, and visited one or two camps to see for himself the conditions about which he had read so much. In a letter home he describes what life was like in Warriner's office with its queues of desperate people asking questions about emigration that frequently couldn't be given a positive answer. Once, he went with an official of a Czech refugee agency to one of the wretched camps to see whether he could "help out". While the official handed out tiny amounts of subsistence money to each family for food, he tried to explain to desperate families how it might be possible to save children before adults. He describes the scene in a letter home:

> But how does one answer such questions as, "How long will it be before my child can go? I know myself it may take months, and maybe they may never be able to go. And what about the question, "And will I soon be able to follow my child?" It may well be that circumstances will prevent her ever seeing her child again if we are successful in getting it to England. And so there is weeping when they can't go, and weeping again when they go and weeping because they don't want to go but only want enough money to exist. And then there is the very big problem of mothers with kids who are far too small to be parted. What is to be done here? Some of these mothers

are already on the streets, driven there by a strong human instinct, that of protecting their young.

The problems appeared quite overwhelming, and the pressure on Winton was increased by the fact that officially his holiday from his stockbroker's office was only two weeks long. Both decision and action had to be fast. What Winton saw almost immediately was that the children had to be his priority because they were nobody else's. For some reason there were children's agencies that were getting hundreds of children out of Germany and Austria, but the same was not true for Czechoslovakia. Here, due to the crisis in the Sudetenland, the focus, as we have seen, was initially on saving the leaders of this region because they were thought to be in real physical danger from vengeful Nazis, and the children were not. Yet at the same time there was a real awareness that many children needed help. At a committee meeting of the BCRC in London as early as January 9, the plight of the Jewish children in Prague had been discussed. Warriner had already become responsible for a large group, some abandoned, some orphaned, some simply separated from their parents in the chaos of the drift of tens of thousands of refugees. She had found places for them to stay, but at this time she had other responsibilities to worry about, so that when Winton appeared on the scene she wasted no time in persuading him to focus on the rescue of children.

What is particularly impressive about the early days of both Warriner's and Winton's relief efforts is the speed that they moved from inexperience and bewilderment at the immensity of the task before them, to positive action. Already mentioned is Warriner's cri de coeur when she first arrived in

Prague, "I had no idea at all what to do, only a desperate wish to do something." Winton's initial reaction was much the same. One minute he is writing home that Warriner wants him to become the Honorary Secretary of a Prague Children's Section, and that he has met all the children's aid agencies; the next minute he is rather apprehensively admitting that "as far as I can see my work with children is only just beginning. I shall very likely have to carry on in London." Then he purloins Warriner's BCRC letterhead from her office and dashes off a letter to his mother asking her to see whether she can discover some of the basic regulations of the refugee emigration business:

> Could you go to the Immigration Section of the Home Office and find out what guarantees you need to bring a child into the country? If a family wishes to guarantee for a child, what do they have to do? If forms have to be filled can you get a few specimens. Is it easier to get children in a block? If so why? And if so how many at a time? Can one get a child over if someone guarantees for a year? If not can one if the guarantee is for two years? What is the shortest guarantee required? Or what is the smallest cash guarantee required?

This tumble of questions illustrates nicely the pressure on a man starting from scratch, but more than ready (to mix a metaphor or two) to clear the decks, roll up his sleeves and dive in.

What was needed first of all was to bring a degree of organization to the various refugee agencies, and luckily organization was Winton's forte. He reckoned that there were five main agencies working in Prague at the time, basically defined by religious affiliation, each therefore with its own preferred client base. One problem was that many refugees in their desperation filled out applications at several agencies and waved these multiple applications in front of harried consular officials. If all of these groups could agree to come together and put their children on one List to be dealt with at one office it would obviously be much more efficient and productive. The trouble was none of the groups were eager to "join up" because they wanted to be assured that their own children would have priority. After two or three days Winton hadn't got very far, and so he resorted to a simple deception. He informed each agency that he now had a list of children that he would be happy to look after, and that they could send him their lists if they wanted to. Or not. The next day he had all five lists and could start on the children's case sheets that he would take back to London with him. Name? Age? Address? Photograph? Relations? Siblings? Financial Contribution? These were probably among the main pieces of information that were required. Very soon he had over 500 files.

And in the midst of all this interviewing and form filling and letter writing, Winton also managed to be involved in the departure of at least one plane load of children during his short stay in Prague. There are some five different descriptions of a group of children flying out of Ruzyne Airport at this time, but it is very hard to decide whether they are independent accounts of the same transport or all different ones. My own guess is that they were of two separate flights, which we may call the Beautiful Swedish Spy Flight, and the Hansi Neumann Flight.

The Beautiful Swedish Spy Flight is worthy of a 1930s film noir. On January 13, Winton went to an ex-pat party where he met someone who knew someone who knew a girl at the Swedish embassy who was said to be looking for children to put on a flight to Sweden. Apparently she was working for the Red Cross. When recalling the incident some fifty years later, he decided she was "the most beautiful girl in Prague." He contacted her the next day and arranged a lunch date. He also invited Doreen Warriner. The lunch was going well, and Winton was in the midst of an enthusiastic description of his refugee plans when he got a kick on the ankle from Warriner followed by a delicate flash of eyebrow semaphore. Later she told him that something had aroused her suspicions and when she'd checked at the Swedish embassy she found that the girl was a German mole. However, Winton pursued the contact. He figured that if her Red Cross cover was genuine and that she really had 30 spaces on a plane, then he didn't care about her political allegiances. In the end the beautiful spy appears to have been harmless and the children left for Sweden. It was Winton's first triumph. Of course at this time he had no money and no organization, and was mainly working out of Warriner's office so we may speculate that the children came from those whom Warriner had been looking after, and had been so desperate for someone to take off her hands. The flight probably left around January 16/17.

An earlier flight was the Hansi Neumann Flight, which left on January 12. This has become the most famous of all the Kindertransports due to one iconic photograph. It is the famous picture of Winton holding the small boy in the striped, knitted cap (See page 38). The boy is three year old Hansi Neumann. In fact this wasn't a transport that had very much to do with Winton. It had been mainly organized by The Barbican Mission to the Jews which had been touting for business in Prague for a few weeks. The Barbican Mission was founded in the 19th century for the express purpose of converting Jews, and its leaders in 1938 saw Prague as an opportunity not to be missed. The entry of a Jewish child into the Christian fold could be exchanged for a ticket to freedom. Most would agree that this pressuring of parents to barter their child's safety for a baptism is graceless, though it seems to have been reasonably effective. The Barbican Mission rescued about 60 children from Prague.

In his notes Winton mentions that this transport was "fixed up" by the Barbican Mission, and that it was "arranged by us". This leaves the division of labour unclear. As has been mentioned, Winton had no organization at this point so presumably the "us" once again refers to Warriner's BCRC office. Since he had no budget, the plane was probably paid for by the Barbican Mission, and Winton may have looked after the logistics. In his diary he describes the event at some length. The media had been alerted, dozens of the children's families and friends were in attendance and a cavalcade of buses had been laid on to travel from the KLM office in Prague out to the airport where as Winton tells us, "for over 1 1/2 hours there was a mixture of complete chaos, high excitement and passionate adieus". And in the midst of it all, he "was photographed in X different positions, holding, leading and helping the children". Several of the shots were with little Hansi. Finally it was time to board the plane, and Winton "posing as a journalist" got on the plane for a few minutes as well. "This of course the parents were not allowed to do, but the final adieus, being made at a distance of some 50 yards, were all the more pathetic. I did not see one of the kids crying." The plane landed at Croydon Airport from where the children were taken by bus to the Barbican Mission's residential home in Brockley. The story has a sad ending.

Hansi's parents disappeared in the concentration camps. Hansi died in the Mission home of an inner ear infection.

By the second week of January the size of the task that he had taken on was apparent to Winton, and he wrote to Geoffrey Hart, his boss at Crews & Co, asking for an extension to the two week holiday which was now fast coming to an end. Mr. Hart replied on January 9 (a Monday) to say that he'd just had a lovely time at his new villa in the South of France, that there seemed to be all sorts of exciting things going on in the world of stocks and shares, and that he'd "sooner you were taking a rest here rather than doing heroic work with thousands of poor devils who are suffering through no fault of their own," and that he expected to see him back at his desk by the following Monday. On Wednesday, Warriner also wrote to Hart pleading for more time for Winton. The refugee organization, she said,

> is now at a very critical point, and if he leaves at the moment I am afraid the whole thing will come to a standstill; could he not possibly remain another two weeks? I am relying on him to organize the chaos which exists here, and then to bring the documents to London. I am very short-handed and have no one else who can take over the work he is doing.... I am extremely grateful to you for letting Mr. Winton come; his energy is absolutely invaluable and he has drawn all the different organizations together in the most amazing way and brought order into chaos....so I hope you will not mind my asking if he can remain until he can hand it over.

Hart, no doubt swamped by worry about his stocks and shares, doesn't appear to have replied. Winton took a further ten days holiday anyway.

Even so, time was running out for Winton. Fortunately he was able to share the load when another Englishman appeared on the scene. This was Trevor Chadwick whose contribution will be examined in more detail later on. He had originally come to Prague to select two boys for the family prep school in Swanage. Having delivered them safely he immediately returned and offered his help, "and from then on, writes Winton, "worked with me for about 18 hours a day until we both returned to England." When Winton finally left Prague on Saturday, January 21, he probably had an extra piece of luggage to carry - a suitcase containing his data base of child refugees, the hundreds of case sheets that he and Chadwick had compiled over the previous days. What he may not have realized as he flew out of Prague was that he'd just finished the easy part of the job. Setting up the London end of the operation would be much more difficult - as Warriner herself knew very well, because there was still no organization for the emigration of the Czech children, and if the BCRC didn't take Winton's fledgling group under its wing, then it probably wouldn't fly.

The day before he left she wrote a letter to Margaret Layton the Hon. Sec. of the BCRC strongly recommending Winton as the man to solve the Kinder problem:

> *Could I suggest that you put the organization of the children refugees from Czechoslovakia in the hands of Winton. He is ideal for the job. He has enormous energy, businessman methods, knows the situation perfectly here. He has prepared the case sheets for several hundred children, collected all the offers, and all that he needs now is authority to go ahead. It is an opportunity for the committee to get the services of a really first class organizer.*

I've been trying for three months to get these children away. Save the Children has disclaimed responsibility, so has Interaid, and our own committee is overburdened with more urgent things. I would be glad if I could delegate this part of the work: and I am sure you would. It could quite well be taken out of the committee's scope, and Winton will get things through if you will give him status as secretary of a children's section.

Our main difficulty is that we do not know how to get permits through the H.O.

The note, which seems to have been dashed off at speed like all Warriner's letters, is nicely symbolic of the obstacles faced by her and her team - the excessive work load, the sense of urgency, the lack of co-operation, the sluggishness of the Home Office, chaos only just being kept at bay. Even the note itself, with its barely legible lettering, suggests that a desperately overused typewriter ribbon needed to be replaced.

As soon as he arrived home Winton went to see Layton, who subsequently wrote to Warriner (January 26) that she thought he would be "very useful to us here". She also passes along the good news that there is a chance that the Home Office will allow batches of applications to be processed for the children, maybe as many as 30 at a time. To Winton, fresh from the frenzy of Prague, this was all very low-key and snail-paced. His main problem was that he had no status, no organization, no title, and to begin with no office, and therefore no springboard for the soliciting of funds. As we have seen, for the BCRC with their remit being the safety of the leaders of the Sudetenland, children were a secondary consideration. The solution, Winton very quickly concluded, was to take matters very much into his own hands. As he explained in an interview he gave fifty years later in Jerusalem, *the BCRC at that time had far too much work to do to be able to cope with the children, so I worked from home and we made notepaper [with the BCRC letterhead] which looked very official, and underneath it we put "Children's Section" with my home address....That's how we started, and then somebody brought me a list of all the various [BCRC] committees throughout England, who were subcommittees of the BCRC in London and so, of course still without their permission, we wrote letters telling them what we were doing and that we wanted to find guarantors for these children to bring them over. And that's really how it started.*

With a home-built organization, the self-appointed title of Hon. Sec., official- looking writing stock, and a crucial list of addresses, Winton was in business. And of course the BCRC took him under their wing fairly quickly. Every day at 3 or 4 o'clock after his work at the Stock Exchange he was in his new office where, with the help of volunteers, letters were churned out to possible guarantors, dossiers sent out about refugee children to possible guardians, money was pleaded for, articles and other publicity was generated, and the Home Office was lobbied for permits. Excerpts from a fundraising letter of May 1939 to "Dear Sir (or Madam)" give the flavour.

It is not generally known that a Committee dealing entirely with Refugee Children from Czechoslovakia is in existence......Up to the end of January last (that is 4 months after Munich) there was no organization in London dealing with the children from Czechoslovakia......From the beginning we worked under very great handicaps.......committees all over England had been formed to deal with Refugees from Germany......All this had resulted in the fact that up to now very little indeed has been done for the children in Czechoslovakia......Their

*condition is appalling.......Memories are short, and people are inclined to forget the misery which was caused when, for example, the plebiscite was cancelled in Sudetenland...
...something must be done quickly to help at least the most urgent cases. Some children must be got out without delay.....At the most, only 200 children have so far left Czechoslovakia....... Guarantors are available, as is evident from the number of children being brought out of Germany. Some of these guarantees must be used for our children...... I have in the office case papers with photos of 5000 children [from which] our office in Prague has selected a list of 250 really desperately urgent cases-.......
Our office in Prague is working well and we can bring any child to this country within 3 weeks of it being guaranteed.....Hoping you will see your way to help us......*

Many years later Winton, perhaps typically, downplayed the effort involved in putting in a full days work at the Stock Exchange, and then going home to drum up business (as he would probably have put it) for the Kindertransports. In the Jerusalem interview he remarks, "Out of 50 million people, 600 odd people saying that they'd take a child isn't such a fantastic business, you know. There are people who will do that." Referring to the whole operation as a fairly simple "business" was typically his way of demystifying his rescue efforts and avoiding emotionalism. In the same interview he explained the adoption process as follows:

*WINTON:.... When somebody said: "We will take a child",
we sent them a picture with eight photos [another version
suggests it was six photos], and a lot of people said you
can't do that. It is an awful way. It is kind of
commercializing it all, but it worked very well because
they looked at this [and said] "we will have that one. It
looks nice.*

INTER: And they chose one?
WINTON: They chose one. It was like running a business.
Awful really but it worked... see here, on the outside was
the name of the child and on the inside...When somebody
chose a child, we just crossed it out, just like running a
business.

Elsewhere in this interview Winton's hard-headed, completely unsentimental approach to his rescue operation is even more marked. At times it is possible to sense a certain impatience with the reverence with which he is being treated. In reply to the question about whether Myra Hess the famous pianist continued to pay for the upkeep of the child she sponsored for the standard £50 he replies, "I don't know. I don't know. I mean quite frankly I was only interested in getting the children to England and I didn't mind a damn what happened to them afterwards, because the worst that would happen to them in England was better than being in the fire." And throughout the interview he continued to hammer home, sometimes one senses to the interviewer's discomfort, that his priority was saving children, and that race and religion were of no concern to him.

- *I was only interested in saving the children and quite frankly I'm not religious.*

- *The Jews, particularly the orthodox Jews were very cross about it, but I was creating a skeleton to bring out children and I didn't mind if the children were Jewish or Communist or Catholic if they were endangered, and I didn't mind who they went to.*

- *I think one of the things that is overlooked, particularly by the Jews is that they say, "Look at all the Jews you've*

saved. This is marvelous." But I didn't set out to save the Jews particularly, although I knew the majority of people I would save would be Jewish, but the idea of bringing out the children was to bring out those who would be endangered when the Germans came, and it wasn't only the Jews by any means.
INTERVIEWER: You mean among these 600 [you saved] there are also non-Jews?
WINTON: Oh yes. Yes. Because as I say, the idea was to save children.

- If somebody said, we've got a guarantor and this is the child they want," I said, "Fine." I didn't go and see the family or anything like one would today.
INTERVIEWER: You are above these things. You didn't go.
WINTON: One tried to find out if the family was suitable, but if the Home Office would accept somebody's guarantee and they had £50 and they would give us a permit to bring the child into England, it didn't much matter if it wasn't a good guarantor. At least they were in England. To my mind that was the only important thing at that point.

Both Winton and Chadwick expressed their regrets that they weren't able to save more children, but it's impossible to tell from the Winton interview whether the problem was a lack of sponsors or the lack of urgency emanating from the Home Office. The seeming placidity of the Home Office was an on-going complaint for all the rescuers. As we've seen, Winton says that it wasn't hard to get 600 sponsors from a country of 50 million people, but elsewhere he states that they would have been more successful "if we'd had more guarantors". What is less clear is whether more guarantors would have produced more entry permits. Doreen Warriner's frustration with what she saw as the impassiveness of the Home Office has already been noted.

Winton seems to have fallen foul of the same culture quite early on. In February he is champing at the bit in his eagerness to get his Children's Section operative, and apparently planning to make overtures to the Home Office on his own. For his temerity as the new boy on the block as it were, he gets a gentle tap on the wrist from the BCRC Hon. Sec. "Mrs Rae tells me that you were thinking of putting permits through the Home Office on your own. It would, I think, be unfortunate if you did this, as the Home Office is always antagonized by a multiplication of applications.

Chadwick also deplored the slowness of the Home Office.

> *They just didn't realize. If only the Home Secretary could have spent a few days with me, seeing brutality, listening to, not arguing with, young Nazis, as I often did, he would doubtlessly have pushed the whole thing along fast. If he had realized that the regulations were, for so many children, the first nudge along the wretched road to Auschwitz, he would, of course, have immediately imported the lot. But that is too much wisdom after the event.*

And Beatrice Wellington, typically the bluntest and most aggressive of the rescuers, didn't mince her words either with the Gestapo or British officialdom, and was probably more comfortable dealing with the former than the latter. When describing the final days of the BCRC in Prague she writes,

> *In the opinion of the British workers who have returned to Prague, the events leading up to their departure clearly show that whatever may have been the cause and whoever may have engineered this move, it was not due to local interference or antagonism on the part of the Gestapo, but rather to machinations arranged by the British authorities.*

But of course it wasn't lack of sponsors or slow government departments that finally ended the rescue efforts. It was September 1, 1939, the day, long expected, when the armies marched and lands were invaded and borders were closed. The day that the largest of the Kindertransports, waited at Prague's Wilson Station with 250 children sitting expectantly in their seats. This train load disappeared into history, and none of the children were heard of again. Fifty years later the memory of this lost transport was still painful for Winton.

> WINTON: ..... *The last transport would have been the biggest. It was due to leave on the first of September. The day war broke out. We had 250 children. 250 foster parents waiting for them in England and not one of them has ever been heard of again. It is not all fun having all this suddenly brought up again.*
> INTERVIEWER: *I understand that most of the relatives or parents of these children perished.*
> WINTON: *Oh yes.*

One can add that it is possible that not all 250 children perished. Some of them, although scheduled for this train, may not in fact have boarded it; others may have been taken off at the last moment. The fate of this final transport remains something of a mystery.

* * *

So now there was nothing left to do in the Children's Section in its Bloomsbury office except tidy up loose ends, pack some boxes with documents, letters and photos, take the boxes home and store them in the attic. Then it was a question of deciding what to do about the war. Winton's first impulse was to be a conscientious objector, and as such he became an air raid warden in Hampstead, and later joined the Red Cross as a driver. In no time he was across the Channel, and shortly after that a part of the retreat to Dunkirk. Back in England he joined the Royal Air Force because, as he explained in the Jerusalem interview,

You can't keep out of it forever. Eventually you get dragged in and there are more important things than your conscience. You want to do something for your country as well. It is all a long time ago.

Due to his poor eyesight he never got to fly combat aircraft; instead he became a Flying Instructor, and at the end of the war the second in command of some sort of travelling R.A.F. exhibition which toured the war-torn cities of Europe. In the Winter of 1945 Winton drove again into Prague, but he does not appear to have been particularly stirred by revisiting the scene of the dramatic events five years earlier. Perhaps he had no wish to remember. In 1947 he took on a job that would have required a strong stomach. He was one of those in charge of recycling or finding a home for the Nazi plunder of the war years; the rugs and art and gems and watches certainly, but also objects with more horrifying associations – rings and gold tooth fillings for example. This period of his life deserves a book of its own.

In 1948, Winton married Grete Gjelstrup, a Danish lady, and returned to England to look for a job. He decided against banking, but instead went into business with such success that he was able to retire when he was 58. In the meantime, he and Grete had three children. The third, Robin, was mentally handicapped and died when he was seven. In his retirement, Winton was able to focus a lot of time and energy on Mencap, and also on Abbeyfield, a charity for the elderly. In 1983 he was awarded an MBE "for services to the community".

The events of Winton's later years have often been recorded. Perhaps the most famous story is that as he was settling into his retirement, content to cultivate his garden and devote time to his charities, he decided one day in his eightieth year to do a much needed clean-out of the loft. Grete was with him when amongst the bric-a-brac they found some worn boxes which contained yellowing, fifty year old papers. And so the Prague Kindertransport story came to light once again. Actually, Winton has hinted that this story has been slightly embellished by a romantically inclined media, but it is true that it was only now that the archival value of the old documents was acknowledged and that they had to be found a better home. The papers were shown to Dr. Elisabeth Maxwell, a holocaust specialist who fortuitously also happened to be the wife of Robert Maxwell, the owner of The Mirror Newspaper Group, and himself, in 1939, a Jewish refugee from Czechoslovakia. Winton was about to become very famous indeed.

Here it is probably necessary to pause for a moment to apologize to anyone who feels that the following pages unfairly diminish Winton's achievements. Unfortunately, such has been the (understandable) adulation that he has received from those he helped, and so embellished has the story become (often as a means of selling a newspaper or attracting a viewing audience) that the truth of history itself has become distorted. In the past Winton himself has frequently tried to correct the more egregious errors, though one sometimes gets the feeling that the strength of the hagiography is such that it must be, for him, a bit like shouting into a gale. What follows, then, may be seen as an attempt to set the record straight and thereby put Winton's extraordinary achievement into a clearer perspective.

The launching of Winton onto the national stage seems to have been carefully planned and orchestrated. It occurred on February 28th, 1988, when Winton was in his eightieth year. That morning The Sunday Mirror published a three page spread under the headline "THE LOST CHILDREN" - a headline which, with its faint overtones of Peter Pan, seems to miss the mark entirely. On the same evening he was featured on the BBC'S "That's Life" . These first two pieces of publicity may be seen as having set the tone and pace for much of the future coverage of the Prague story. For example, it is in The Daily Mirror that we first see the well-known photograph of Winton carrying Hansi Neumann, the little boy in the striped cap. This image has become a defining one and appears in many a book and blog, but as has already been mentioned, Hansi was not actually a "Winton child". A sub-headline in the article reads, "Little Refugees left waiting for their brave Pied Piper". This might have puzzled some of the more literate readers of this tabloid even more than the Peter Pan reference - considering that the Pied Piper story is about an act of child abduction motivated entirely by revenge due to money. Catchy, but wholly inappropriate, titles would later become an embarrassment to Winton, most obviously the ludicrous Schindler of Britain/England tags that became attached to him. The article also starts the myth that Winton more or less acted alone, that he became "a Committee of One" in the rescue of the children, an assertion that could hardly be further from the truth.

That same evening the T.V. "That's Life" programme was a veritable coup de theatre. Winton was of course the guest of honour, but a guest of honour who had no idea what was in store for him. No doubt he expected that there would be a brief but enthusiastic retelling of the Prague refugee story, and how he raised money all those years ago from his London office, and managed to find guarantors for the children, and so on. He was seated in the middle of the front row of the studio audience, but he was completely unaware that the people who sat on either side of him and behind him, and indeed throughout the audience, were former Kinder, the transport children of fifty years earlier whom he didn't know and had never met before. It was the perfect emotional ambush, stage- managed with the usual Rantzen flair. Needless to say it was a moment of the highest sentimentality when the ladies on either side of him introduced themselves, and then the rest of the audience made itself known with a standing ovation. No doubt Rantzen was delighted that she had managed to get her normally shy and retiring guest to put a finger behind his glasses in order to wipe away a tear. It was one of her more memorable "That's Life" programmes; it is also reported by Vera Gissing that though Winton "was happy to meet the children....he wasn't happy about how it was done".

During the next decade or so the accolades increased in volume and grew in number. In May 1989 Winton went to Jerusalem as an honoured guest and to deposit his documents in the Yad Vashem archives. Only the technicality that he was of Jewish parentage prevented him from being honoured as one of the Righteous Among the Nations. In 1991 he returned to Prague where he was given the freedom of the city and granted an audience with Vaclav Havel the President of Czechoslovakia. In 1998 he was awarded the Masaryk Medal, one of the highest awards of the state.

1999 saw the premiere of Matej Minac's All My Loved Ones, starring Rupert Graves as Nicholas Winton. In 2002 Minac also put out a documentary called "Nicholas Winton: The Power of Good" which won an Emmy. The same year saw the publication of Muriel Emanuel and Vera Gissing's excellent *Nicholas Winton and the Rescued Generation*. Gissing's contribution is a detailed and deeply felt tribute to the man who became her friend and neighbour. The book also discusses the contributions of Warriner and Chadwick, and though Beatrice Wellington doesn't get the coverage she deserves this is probably because the facts weren't available. On the other hand Barazetti receives more coverage than he deserved but, again, this is because many facts were not then known. In December 2002 Winton received a knighthood.

During all these years there were, of course, literally dozens of articles in newspapers and journals and the ubiquitous blog about Winton's exploits, and it is here that the history of the Prague Kindertransports in general, and Winton's contribution in particular, became increasingly distorted. How and why this happened is an interesting study in its own right. It is a phenomenon that frequently occurs during the incubation of a myth. We crave Heroes, (and prefer to ignore Brecht's counter comment, "Pity the country that needs heroes!") and almost always we prefer to focus our wonderment and our adulation on a single figure. More than one hero tends to confuse us, and as far as the media is concerned it dissipates interest. And so each story gets a single hero. This improves viewing figures and increase circulations. Unfortunately, the media of whatever sort also finds it hard to distinguish between heroism and hagiography, and since the profits are in direct proportion to the hagiographic hyperbole, the central figure becomes endowed with more impressive attributes and credited with greater feats. These are typically borrowed from secondary characters in the story who therefore slowly fade into the background. To some extent this process is what has happened here, though it needs to be emphasized that such an outcome was absolutely beyond Winton's own control. Frequently bewildered and irritated, he has time and again tried to set the record straight, but without much success. And so it is that the assertions about his achievements proliferate. The sort of claims that are made on his behalf are well known. News stories and the like variously claim that,

"he arranged for the children to travel through Hitler's Germany"

"he arranged for 669 children to get out of the country on eight trains."

"he spent only a couple of months in Prague."

"he arranged safe passage for more than 650 children."

"he saved 669 children from a transport to Nazi death camps by taking them to London."

" he left on the last departure of the special trains that he'd hired at his own expense."

"he was an amazingly heroic individual who demonstrated courage."

"he almost single-handedly saved the children."

"he spirited the children away from the Nazis on eight trains."

"in 1938 he had an intuition, and not many people had this intuition, that there was a really dangerous situation. ...which nobody recognized at that time."

And so the claims roll on.

Because these misconceptions are so deeply embedded in the Winton story, the facts are worth re-iterating. It is certainly not true that "not many people" realized that there was a "really dangerous situation" in Prague. It was common knowledge and dozens flocked there in 1938 to see whether they could help, Winton amongst them. He was probably fortunate to fall under the wing of Doreen Warriner who had arrived two months earlier. He was in Prague for no longer than about three weeks, and of course had left long before the German army of occupation arrived. Subsequently his area of operations was an office in Bloomsbury from where he conducted the crucial contacts with the Home Office and the all-important search for sponsors. He therefore had nothing to do with the travel arrangements of the children, which were all conducted from the Prague end. He accompanied no trains, he arranged no safe passages for any children, and he spirited no children away from the Nazis. It becomes equally obvious, of course that he was far from being "a committee of one", or that he "almost single-handedly saved the children". Indeed, as he says quite bluntly in the Jerusalem interview, "I had no connection with the children". And it follows, of course, that he "chose" none of them. As he says, "exactly how they were chosen in Prague, I don't know".

Perhaps all these misconceptions are encapsulated most dramatically in the film mentioned above, All My Loved Ones. The film focuses on the fictitious Silberstein family, a well-to-do Jewish family who live in a country house outside Prague. They do not believe that the arrival of the Germans will make any difference to their way of life ("the Nazis are much too louche to be taken seriously") until it is too late. In the end only the son of the family escapes. At the beginning of the story proper there is a brief introduction to a character called Nicholas Winton. In the final scene, a reconstruction of the departure of the last Kindertransport from Wilson station, this character appears again in a sort of supervisory capacity, walking up and down the platform and checking on the children. But as we have seen, the real Winton did none of these things. In all probability he never set foot on the platforms of either of Prague's stations, and he certainly wasn't present during the embarkation of the children (though he welcomed them when they arrived at Liverpool St. station the next day). In short, what Minac, the director, has done is, in time-honoured moviedom fashion, clothed his fictional Winton in the clothes of the historical person who actually did the rough work at the Prague end of the rescue operation. This was Trevor Chadwick. According to Vera Gissing, Winton was initially reluctant to be the central figure in the film. "Surely the story is strong enough to stand on its own", Nicky reasoned. "Why use it in a fictional film?" But the persuasiveness of the eager director eventually overcame the reluctance of the octogenarian. And perhaps none of this should matter. After all, we are all used to the freedom with which films play fast and loose with historical fact in order to boost the box office. We all remember "How America won the war" movies and "How America broke the Enigma code" and so on. This film is perhaps a bit more dishonest because it is book-ended with a Prologue and an Epilogue which feature the "real" Nicholas Winton. The coda consists of an edited version of the "That's Life" programme mentioned earlier. Here, as we've seen, the "real" Winton is shown being feted by an audience of former Kinder, but the juxtaposition of the real with the fabrications of the movie has the effect of validating the latter. It is unlikely that those who see the movie would not come away with the belief that what they have seen in the movie is a fair representation of what Winton actually did in the rescue operation. And so it is that myths flourish.

I should add as a footnote to the above observations, that a short while ago (September 2009) the so-called "Winton Train" made its epic journey from Prague to Liverpool St. Station in memory of the Kindertransports. The web subsequently had more than ten pages of reports about this journey from a variety of sources, that is, well over 100 items. Of these seventy percent referred to "the British Schindler", or some variant, and none of them, with one exception mentioned that anyone else was involved in this enterprise, thus leaving the distinct impression that it was all managed by Winton alone! One can only smile sadly.

Finally we can say that Winton didn't exhibit "courage" or "heroism" in the normally accepted meanings of these words. Such virtues were irrelevant to the job he had to do. Fortunately he had other attributes that were considerably more valuable - tenacity, efficiency, indomitability, integrity and persuasiveness. His weapons were a desk, a typewriter, a letterhead and many volunteers. With the help of a large supporting cast, he was the architect of a splendid plan to save the lives of 669 children. Indeed we may say that the whole of Winton's life has been marked by service to others. The remarkable efforts he made on behalf of the children of Prague, and his later work for Mencap and Abbeyfield have earned him well deserved accolades. And this is the reason why it is so important to avoid all the exaggerations and embellishments of his story as well as the essentially foolish comparisons with Schindlers and Pimpernels. The foolishness reflects on Winton himself and because they are so obviously ridiculous they belittle him. His life needs no false analogies.

TREVOR CHADWICK

I must begin this chapter with a conflict of interest disclaimer because Trevor Chadwick was my father. I don't remember him very well. I have always been envious (and maybe a little sceptical) of those who recall their childhoods with startling clarity, and are able to report the conversations of the nursery and the favourite toys of the sandbox in minute detail. Strain though I might I find that I can conjure up only a few very blurred flashes from the memory bank of my early years, and none of them includes my father.

When the war began the family school in Swanage where we lived was evacuated to Penn House in Buckinghamshire. This large estate with its many kempt lawns and fish ponds and sprawling woods was a paradise for children. One day, when I think I was about six, the assistant head master told me that my father was in a secluded corner of the grounds and wanted to say hello. I remember almost nothing about the meeting. I think I can "see" a figure in uniform, either naval or R.A.F. I assume now that he came to say goodbye because he was leaving the family, but I have no recollection of what was said or of my reaction one way or another. This is not surprising when one remembers that the school was my family, that I was surrounded by friends and relations, and that my father had not featured strongly in my life before this. Nor would I have felt different or left out in any way. None of the other boys saw much of their fathers in those days.

Trevor Chadwick (1907-1979) with his older son, Charles, on a boat in Poole harbour c. 1935.

And that was the last I saw of him for about thirty years. There was no correspondence. When I left school I emigrated to Canada, went to university, got married, had children and started teaching at university myself. Often we would come to England in the summer for holidays or extended periods of study, and it was while on one of these that word came from Oslo, where Trevor lived with his third wife, Sigi, that he would like to meet while they were on a trip to London. An understandable curiosity was, I think, my main reaction to this proposal. To meet someone called "my father" after a thirty year silence, someone I didn't know at all, was certainly intriguing. And perhaps it was made a little spicier by the remembrance that when I was growing up I was sometimes admonished for bad behaviour with the phrase, "Just like your father!" Would that have made me like him or dislike him? I'll have to leave this one to the trick cyclists (as he used to call them). But what I can say with certainty was that there was absolutely no sense of resentment for the past. The meeting itself, I told myself would be calm and composed. In the event it was quite fiery. For some reason I went out to Heathrow Airport to meet them. Though I was very nervous, I was determined to be cool and welcoming. I was wearing a duffel coat. Unfortunately I had a book of matches in the coat pocket and my hand in this pocket betrayed my calmness. As the moment of meeting approached my fingers started rubbing the matches together quite agitatedly, and they burst into flames just as they appeared. So that is how the thirty year separation ended. A bemused father watching his son slapping dementedly at smoke issuing from his clothing. It was a way of breaking the ice.

I met him maybe four more times during our intermittent

trips to England; a visit to London Zoo, a posh restaurant, and then when he and Sigi returned to England to live, two trips to Southampton where they'd retired. The memories are more vivid now. On the last occasion he was in a wheelchair having had a leg amputated after incompetent nursing in a local hospital, and we wheeled him to the pub. When it came time to leave he made a scene, and our exit was a little embarrassing. Apparently alcohol had always been something of a problem for him. He died in 1979. At his funeral I remember thinking that though I knew very little about him and hadn't seen him very often I was pleased that he was my father. He was intelligent and he was funny and I'd heard a persistent rumour that he'd helped to rescue quite a few children in Prague just before the war. The reader will have to judge for him or herself from all these reminiscences whether my evaluation of his contribution to this rescue effort is unbiased. I have no doubt that it is.

* * *

Trevor Chadwick was born on April 22, 1907, the third of four children. His father died when he was five years old. It was openly agreed by all members of the family that he became his mother's favourite and was horribly spoilt. He was the only one of the four children, for example, who went on to Oxford (having attended the Dragon School and Sedbergh to which he'd won a scholarship) where he captained the Corpus Christi rugby team, and ran up debts, probably on bar bills and horse races, and was constantly bailed out by his mother after furious rows, according to family anecdote. He graduated in 1928 with a Third in Jurisprudence. It is thought that he should have done better than this. On graduation he had two obvious possible choices of career. One was to teach at Forres, the prep school in Swanage that his father had founded, now being run by his uncle, Rev. R.M. Chadwick; the other was to do Something Else. He chose Something Else, joined the Colonial Service and was posted to Nigeria as a district officer. He served there for about eighteen months. His time in Africa was possibly curtailed by his desire to get married. Before he went to Nigeria, he had often visited his younger brother, Hugh, who was working for a farmer near Battle. The farmer had a beautiful daughter, and we may guess that she was as much the object of his visits as was his brother. They were married in 1931, and because he didn't want to subject his new wife to a rough and lonely life in a rather unhealthy part of the world, he left the Service and went to the family school, where he taught Latin and other subjects.

To begin with there was a hope that he would eventually take over the headmastership of the school, but it soon became clear that his erratic life-style, made him unsuitable for such a life. A distaste for convention, for rules, for etiquette, and a dislike of any sort of pomp and circumstance can be attractive characteristics; they can also spill over into irresponsibility. He became a member of the Swanage lifeboat crew, a position of which he was very proud. He is easily recognizable in the photograph of the 1930's crew that hangs in the lifeboat shed today. He had a particularly close bond with Bob Brown, the coxswain of the lifeboat and landlord of The Black Swan, who later became chairman of the Swanage Town Council. Bob Brown related how Trevor wanted to learn to sail: "If I learned him to sail, he'd learn me to drive. He bought a 16-foot Weymouth dinghy to race in Swanage Bay, and on racing days he'd learn me out in the car first, and then we'd take them L plates and fix 'en to the shrouds." Quite often he went off lobster fishing with Bob Brown, and quite often this activity overlapped with his teaching. The story is that there were many occasions when he turned up in the classroom in his fisherman's jersey, and there were times when he didn't turn up at all. In other words, alcohol was sometimes a problem. As Bob Brown remarked, "When I was shutting up the pub for the night I knew who would be creeping in the back door. He was just like one of the family." The school tolerated all this, but it must have been difficult for the headmaster to have as a staff member a nephew who served behind the bar at the local. There are many exotic and possibly apocryphal "Trevor stories" from this period, such as the occasion that he turned up at the school with his head shaved bald for some reason, and the Parent's Day when he appeared as an Italian ice cream vendor and sold ice cream to bemused parents.

But to set beside these eccentricities, Peter Chadwick, who also later became the headmaster of Forres and like his father took holy orders, maintains that above all he was remembered for his kindness. For example he arranged bus trips for the townspeople to attend sporting events, and organized parties for disadvantaged children. Peter particularly remembers him pushing Sergeant Cooper (formerly the school's sports instructor) around in his wheelchair when he was dying of cancer. On one occasion an old man turned up in Swanage looking for Trevor Chadwick who before the war had helped him bring his damaged boat into Swanage Bay. They'd gone off to the Black Swan (where else?) and when the man returned to his boat a good deal later he found that Chadwick had arranged for it to be repaired - without a word having been said about it. But though he may have been generous towards many he appears not always to have extended the same thoughtfulness to his own family. His wife often found life difficult with a man of such unruly habits. From her perspective "his life was pubbing", and her analysis of his main friendships sounds quite astute: "His close friends were the local fishermen - he preferred that type and they hero-worshipped him. Perhaps he needed the worship of these less educated people."

Through the latter part of 1938 the plight of the mainly Jewish children of Germany, Austria and Czechoslovakia was well publicized in England and many appeals for sponsorship circulated, particularly through various church networks. One such appeal arrived on the desk of Rev R.M. Chadwick, and he decided to take two boys into the school. Shortly after Christmas Trevor Chadwick and Geoff Phelps, the sports master, flew to Prague. One can guess with a fair degree of confidence that one of the first people they met was Doreen Warriner, who would have introduced them to the larger refugee situation, and shortly afterwards to Nicholas Winton. As Winton recalls,

> *A young Englishman met me in my hotel one day. Trevor Chadwick had heard about the plight of the refugees and offered to throw up his job as a teacher and come out to help. Two days after our meeting he flew back to England with two refugee boys....The next day he was back in Prague and from then on worked with me for about 18 hours a day until we both returned to England. Later, when we had got things moving in London and I needed someone to look after the Prague end, I took up Trevor's offer.*

Chadwick, in his account of these days in Gershon's We Came As Children, doesn't mention this meeting with Winton. It is the desperate situation of the refugees that strikes him most forcibly. "We got a clear impression of the enormity of the task. We so often saw halls full of confused refugees and batches of lost children, mostly Jewish, and we saw only the fringe of it all. Soon after our return I felt that I had to do more about it."

In the end, the two men took three children to England. A girl, Gerda Mayer, who was sponsored by Chadwick's mother, and who became a very fine poet, and the two boys for the school, Willi Weigl and Peter Walder. I remember them well, especially Willi who became one of my playmates.

It is difficult to give precise dates for Chadwick's movements in Prague. In his Gershon recollections he gives no dates, so it is a question of trying to mesh the events he describes with those that Winton describes while remembering that both men are writing about events that happened thirty or more years earlier. From Winton's statement (above) we can see that the two men worked together until Winton flew back to London on January 21,1939. It sounds as though Chadwick left at about the same time, but then the uncertainties begin. Winton, in the above quotation, says, "Later, when "we" had got things moving in London...." Are we to understand from this that the two men continued to work on the organizational aspects of the transports and sponsors, and so on, in London? Chadwick leaves a different impression. "Soon after our return....I went to Friends' House and later to the Movement for the Care of Children from Germany. They were busy finding guarantors, and I flew back to Prague to find children who would fit in with the guarantors' wishes." Perhaps memory was at fault here, but what we can say is that some time in February Chadwick had agreed to look after the Prague end of the Kindertransport initiative. What he did during the missing weeks of January and February remains unclear, though we should remember that he also had some personal issues to resolve before he could finally establish himself in Czechoslovakia. For example he had rather suddenly and at the last minute left his teaching job which surely must, to some extent, have made life difficult at the school. Could he even have taught for the first week or two of the new term while a replacement was found. And then there was his family which he seems to have been in the process of leaving. Presumably arrangements needed to be put in place to safeguard their well-being.

There is one other possibility that is contained in a letter Winton wrote on March 28, 1999, to Gerda Mayer a former Kind, explaining how the transports began:

> *Trevor came out and offered his help and we set up an office together and he agreed to run the Czech side, if, on my return to England, I was able to make workable arrangements with the Home Office. This I was able to do and my job then was to find suitable families which fulfilled the Home Office conditions of entry. Trevor then went to work and dealt with all the considerable problems at the Prague end and this work he continued to carry on even when it became more difficult and dangerous when the Germans arrived. He deserves all praise.*

The implication seems to be that Chadwick waited to see whether Winton could get his madcap scheme of rescuing hundreds of children under way before committing himself, and perhaps meanwhile he did some similar relief work, perhaps for the Quakers. And here it might be worth saying something about the working relationship between these two men. Some of the reports leave the impression that Winton "appointed" Chadwick to the Prague position, that he was in effect the senior partner in the enterprise. This is unlikely to have been the situation. It is worth remembering that Chadwick, now 32, was the older man by some two years. As a colonial officer he would have acted as a magistrate, and dealt with many cases that exercised his judgement and authority; as a school teacher it may have been more a case of scolding small boys; on the Swanage lifeboat there must have been a few stormy nights that would have tested his character. We may say that Winton was the mastermind of the Prague Kindertransports (probably with Warriner's encouragement) but he and Chadwick came together as equals. Indeed, they appear to have formed the perfect partnership; Winton at a desk in London wrestling with the bureaucracy of the Home Office et. al., and Chadwick out in the field in Prague calming the traumas of parents and children at a time of great emotional turmoil.

Chadwick was probably in place in Prague by the end of February, 1939. We can guess this because on March 2nd Winton was sent a telegram signed jointly by Warriner and Chadwick. If we conjecture that it would have taken a day or two for these two to have become reacquainted and familiar enough with each other to send a joint, congratulatory telegram, then we can tentatively suggest a date in late February for his arrival in Prague to start work on the Kindertransports. According to Doreen Warriner, his first group of children left by plane on March 10th and consisted of children she had collected over the previous few weeks and had been stockpiling in the YWCA. This planeload doesn't appear on the "official" list of the Prague Kindertransports, but Chadwick remembered it well because it was his first rescue effort:

> *I took my first air transport rather proudly, on a twenty-seater plane. They were all cheerfully sick, enticed by the little paper bags, except a baby of one who slept peacefully in my lap the whole time—Then there was the meeting with the guarantors - my baby was cooed over and hustled off, and the other nineteen were shyly summing up their new parents, faces alive with hope for the love they were obviously going to be given. I felt depressed as I returned to Prague. Only twenty!*

Rumour had it in Swanage that Chadwick financed this first plane out of his own pocket by selling his boat and his two cars, but this sounds unlikely. As his wife said later, "We never had two cars!". And a second hand Weymouth 14 foot sailboat wouldn't have fetched much on the open market. If there is any truth in the story then it is possible that Chadwick's mother helped to charter the plane, but since Doreen Warriner by now had funds, as we have seen, for refugee relief we may guess that she had a hand in this transport. As she says, "On the 10th [March] a special plane took my children from the YWCA to England, through Winton's organization, by now in charge of Trevor Chadwick."

He was lent an office on Rubesova St. by a Czech cabinet minister which was handily situated a block or two from Wilson Station. He had two assistants, very likely volunteers. One was a 16 year-old Prague girl called Ruth Reser, who herself managed to get out of Prague and eventually reached New York. As the main conduit for refugee children trying to get to England, life was hectic at the office. As he wrote later,

The whole day, from 7 until 7, with twenty minutes for lunch, were taken up with interviewing, filing and writing letters to the guarantors, which perforce could not be scrappy. I can't say how many children were on my books, but it must have been in the thousands. Nor can I say how many I eventually got away, but it was only hundreds, alas.

But it wasn't the paperwork that was the difficult part of the job. Much, much harder to deal with were the emotional stresses of the seemingly endless line of families, the parents frightened, desperate, pleading for help, the children bewildered and miserable that apparently they were to be separated from mother and father. And then there were the times, and there must have been plenty of them, when help had to be refused for one reason or another - perhaps because the child was too old or too young, or because no guarantor had been found, or because the Lists were full, or there was no further room on the transport. But, like Winton, we don't know what criteria Chadwick used in choosing who should go and who should not, but if he had, as he said, "thousands" on his books, there must have been many difficult scenes. And perhaps worst of all would have been the moments of departure on the platforms of Wilson station. There are many reports of the tears and the misery of these occasions, at the attempts at brave faces and cheerful words, and the last minute hugs and clutches. One can only guess at the emotional strain, that continued week after week and month after month, for those involved in this rescue work.

But it appears that Chadwick possessed the best antidote for such strains and tensions. It is interesting that each one of the refugees who remembered these traumatic days in later life all mention Chadwick's sense of humour or general cheerfulness. He was clearly someone who could put people at their ease. Ingeborg Pedelty remembers going for an interview with her mother and sister

> *with a Mr. Chadwick. My memory is of a smiling man who put my very nervous mother at her ease. I don't know in what language the interview was conducted, but at one point Mr. Chadwick mimed that he needed to consult a BIG book. He then pulled out the smallest book I had ever seen (presumably a dictionary). He made us all laugh.*

Margit Fazakerley remembers Chadwick well.

> *How could I forget the man who held my hand (he seemed to have such big hands) sat me on his knee and wiped away my tears. And then there was a darkened room somewhere where we (the children) sat on the floor, "the Chadwick" on a chair teaching us to sing "Baa Baa Black Sheep". My mother told me he was a good and kind man who would take me to England, and that I must be very good and obedient and wait for her until she came for me. Can you imagine the trust and faith and immense gratitude all our parents must have felt towards this tall stranger who could take us all to safety. Only when I grew up and had children of my own did I come to understand how much "the Chadwick" had really done for us. All my family know about him, and as my daughter once said to me, "So you realize mummy that if it were not for Trevor Chadwick, I wouldn't exist.*

During his interview, young Henry Schermer got tied up in the words of his travel documents and began to mispronounce them much to Chadwick's amusement, and he "broke out into merry laughter", and Gerda Mayer can still remember

Chadwick, on the flight over to England, entertaining a three year old child with a hand puppet. Doreen Warriner also enjoyed his company. These two formed a close working partnership, even though ostensibly Warriner's remit was primarily the adult refugees and Chadwick's the children. On March 30th, for example, we find Chadwick helping out when Warriner is preparing sandwiches for the transport she is about to see off. "Trevor Chadwick and I spent a happy hour packing food for seventy, and carried it to the Wilson station." And when she is about to leave for the station to catch the train that will take her from Prague for the last time, her final chat is with Chadwick. "We talked on the terrace of the Legation, where the magnolias were coming out in the sun against the dirty melting snow of March." His talent for laughter and sociability that had made him so popular in the pubs of Swanage had found another, more valuable outlet.

Other Fish To Fry. But then sometime around the beginning of June, after he had got about five transports off, Chadwick left. Why he did so is a complete mystery for which there are a bewildering number of possible explanations. In his memoir in Karen Gershon's *We Came As Children*, he wrote as follows:

> But in the evenings I had other fish to fry that did not have anything to do with children. It became obvious to me as summer developed that certain of my movements were at least suspect and that [the Gestapo] might turn sour. This would jeopardize the children, so I explained these things to London and they arranged a replacement. I shall always have a feeling of shame that I didn't get more out.

If we are to take this literally he is saying that he was

involved with "some other business", that it took place specifically "in the evening", and that it had nothing to do with his children's transports. What most obviously comes to mind is that it had something to do with the forging of travel documents with which, as we have seen, most of the aid workers were involved. These forgeries were mainly for the illegal adult refugees, and thus he was doing it to help Doreen Warriner, but if the necessity arose he was himself perfectly ready to create false documents for his children. His second train transport was, he admits, "illegal". The British Home Office were dragging their feet, and the entry visa documents didn't arrive. In the passage already quoted (See page 30) from Karen Gershon's *We Came As Children*, he describes his career as amateur forger.

Was it in the evenings, then, that Chadwick visited his friendly neighbourhood forger for the latest batch of exit visas or Home Office fakes? Or perhaps involved himself with the underground railway escapes that Warriner had initiated? What is certain is that by May 1939 the Gestapo knew a lot about these forgeries and the illicit transports, and were getting very cross indeed. As we know, Warriner and her helpers had had to leave the country, and it is possible that if Chadwick was found to be implicated this would have jeopardized the Kindertransports. This would have been a pity, particularly because he had managed to forge a smooth working relationship with the Gestapo. However, none of this explains why, if he is quite happy to write about his career as a forger thirty years after the events, he was evasive about the fish he was frying in the evening.

Another possibility put forwards by someone knowledgeable about the murky world of spies, is that it would have been amazing if Chadwick, known to be working in a hotspot like Prague in these pre-war months, where he was quite likely to hobnob with the Gestapo (as he did), a man with the impeccable qualifications of being a middle class, Oxford graduate, a schoolmaster, and ex colonial service officer, had *not* been approached by M.I.6 and, "I say old boy, would you mind keeping your ears and eyes open and if you see anything interesting letting one of our...." And so on and so forth. Such a scenario would certainly tie in with Chadwick's comment quoted above, "It became obvious to me as summer developed that certain of my movements were at least suspect, and that B. and his boys [the Gestapo] might turn sour. This would jeopardize the children...." Interestingly, he does seem to have been debriefed by M.I. 5 when he got home, but unfortunately these files for Prague 1939 seem to have been culled. This theory accounts for the fear of being found out by the Gestapo, and the fact that it had nothing to do with the children, but it doesn't explain why whatever it was that had to be done took place in the evening. If he had any information to impart he could have gone to the British Legation at any time and told the resident spook. On the other hand, there might be some merit in the suggestion that it would be in the evenings that one would visit bars and pubs and mingle with the enemy – in the Gershon book he figures that the precious visas would have been much more readily available if the Home Secretary "could have spent a few days with me, seeing brutality, listening to, not arguing with, young Nazis, as I often did".

More insidious is the accusation that he had become much too friendly with the Germans, and indeed that he had been "turned" by them. In short, that he had become a Nazi lover. It is hard to say where this charge originated, but one theory is that one of the other relief workers, possibly from Sweden, had observed him laughing and joking with the Gestapo brass, and drew the wrong conclusions. In "The Winter in Prague" Warriner, who would have known the situation at first hand, says that the Gestapo "sensed in him a possible convert and he led them on". The second-in-command of the Gestapo in Prague was von Boemelberg whom we have met in an earlier chapter. He was a large, elderly man, probably homosexual who liked his food and drink, and was generally quite a pleasant individual. Indeed, we must remember that these were the days before the film noir war movies where all Gestapo agents wore blank-eyed spectacles, black gloves, long leather coats and had little horns on the sides of their heads. Von Boemelberg seemed friendly enough, and Chadwick wasn't the only one who found him amenable. Stopford also had quite a few dealings with him, and, as he says,

> *had got on working terms with him. He was, I believe, a former Private Secretary of one of the Stinnes family, who, having got into trouble for anti-Nazi activities, was found a safe billet in the Gestapo, with the help of friends!*

A society Nazi, perhaps. Stopford even goes so far as to suggest that Boemelberg indirectly tipped him off when the name of a "wanted" refugee came up so that he could pass it on to Warriner who would make sure that he escaped on her underground railway. In Chadwick's memory,

> *Kriminalrat Boemmelburg (sic) was an elderly, smiling gentleman, far from sinister, who eventually proved a great help, sometimes unwittingly. He was really interested in my project, and his only Nazi-ish remark was a polite query why England wanted so many Jewish children.*

But the question seems to have arisen as to who was the unwitting dupe of whom? Was it Chadwick who was able to manipulate von Boemelburg with his charm, and his fake apologies, or "grovelling" as he puts it, when he included someone illegal on one of his transports, and generally bent over backwards to keep the Kriminalrat happy so that "he agreed to stamp my lists of children for transport without delay"? Or was it Boemelburg who was playing a much dirtier game than the innocent Englishman realized. Joe Schlesinger has this story in his book "Time Zones".

> *Then one day the German [presumably this is Boemelburg] proposed to Chadwick that the refugee committee send back to Prague some of the "politicals" among the adults it had brought to Britain. The Gestapo man assured Chadwick that he would personally guarantee the freedom and safety of all those who returned. Winton was appalled. To accept the Gestapo offer was, of course, impossible; the returnees were certain to be arrested. But to refuse was to endanger the whole rescue operation. Winton blamed Chadwick for allowing himself to be hoodwinked and used by the Gestapo. He recalled him to London.*

On the face of it this story is incomprehensible. One has to wonder why the Gestapo thought that the "refugee committee" in London, in other words the BCRC, a volunteer organization with no government status, would have any authority whatsoever to "send back to Prague" someone who had already made his way to England. Whether they might or might not be arrested if they returned is irrelevant. It is also difficult to see why the Kindertransports would have been endangered if the Gestapo's impossible request was ignored.

If Chadwick left, his replacement could have been faced with the same demand. In fact the transports continued to operate smoothly and without any problems for the next two or three months. Furthermore, it isn't explained in what way Chadwick was "hoodwinked and used" by the Gestapo. It sounds as though blackmail is involved, but it isn't clear what this blackmail might have entailed. And we have to repeat that no matter what lay behind the possible blackmail Chadwick would still have been unable to do anything about the Gestapo's supposed demands. It is perhaps also worth commenting that Chadwick was not an employee of Winton's and therefore wouldn't have been "recalled" to London. He made his own decision and asked for a replacement.

These are some of the theories that might account for the frying of fish in the evenings. Was Chadwick a hoodwinker, or was he hoodwinked? Was he a mole or a forger? Or, as seems most likely, was his smuggling of illegals on the underground railway in danger of being discovered? Or was it none of these things? Perhaps the expression was a throwaway metaphor of no particular significance. We will probably now never know what lay behind his premature departure. However, it is possible to give a tentative date for this departure. By June 1939, it must be remembered, the BCRC refugee effort as originally conceived back in October of 1938, was winding down. Doreen Warriner and her two assistants had all had to leave in April. The BCRC itself had metamorphosed into the CRTC, a government controlled committee. Walter Creighton had been appointed to manage the relief work. He was a civil servant about whom little is known. His few letters indicate that he was keen to close down most of the refugee work. By June the Gestapo and the Jewish Institute had made it clear that they wanted to control all of the Jewish emigration and that the British aid workers were not welcome and should pack their bags and leave. Soon there were only two left, Beatrice Wellington and Trevor Chadwick. Maybe it was this change in the character, outlook and personnel of the refugee aid agencies that contributed to Chadwick's decision to leave. As for the actual date of his departure, we have a letter from Beatrice Wellington to Margaret Layton that begins, "I am taking advantage of Chadwick's journey to send you this", and we also have what looks like a sort of inter office memo from Chadwick to Layton, scrawled on office paper, that begins, "Here is a letter from Miss Wellington." Wellington's letter is dated June 4'h, 1939, so we may cautiously assume that Chadwick left Prague at the beginning of June. There was a Kindertransport on June 2nd, so it is reasonable to conjecture that he saw off this train with its 123 children on board and then left. And perhaps it is worth mentioning that though he wasn't there, the system that he had set up continued to operate apparently with great efficiency. As he says in his memoir when describing how he forged Home Office documents, he couldn't wait any longer because the children were waiting and "the next transport was taking shape." This underlines the obvious point that these train journeys were not stitched together overnight. An enormous amount of forward planning had to go into their organization, from contacting the families, marshalling the children, putting them all on standby, handling hundreds of documents and so on. The next transport after Chadwick's departure took a month to get ready. This was probably because it was the biggest of all the transports (241 children) and Chadwick and his two helpers must have done much of the preliminary organizing. Interestingly we have documents that give us a good idea of the sort of lead-in time refugees required. On June 26th Paul Meisl (Marom) is told,

> *We have your letter from the 24th and inform you that your guarantor has yet to agree to the stipulations of the British Refugee Committee.... When all formalities have been completed we will be informed and put your children on the next transport.*

On July 21 Herr Meisl received another letter which told him,

> *your children Hugo and Rudolf are on the list which has just arrived from London. The transport is expected to leave on July 25th. Please confirm the receipt of this ticket immediately....*

The exchange from Meisl's first enquiry to the departure of the transport has taken one month. It is interesting that both letters are still under the name of T. Chadwick, Hon. Sec., but perhaps this means that no one had yet bothered to change the letterhead.

* * *

Shortly after war was declared, Chadwick joined the Royal Navy Reserve. His boat was H.M.S Mollusc. This was a strange posting. The Mollusc was an ancient steam yacht that originally belonged to the Guinness family, and had been requisitioned by the navy and fitted with a gun. She was stationed off the Tyne, which was thick with shipping and therefore a popular hunting ground for U-boats and the Luftwaffe. She was supposedly a first line of defense for the submarine pens up the Blyth inlet. It was an optimistic role for which the expression "sitting duck" would seem to be appropriate. Chadwick left the ship after five months. A year later she was sunk and still lies in 30 metres of water, a favourite wreck for the diving fraternity.

Almost immediately he joined the Royal Air Force, did an officers' training course and took up administrative duties as a Flying Officer. In the summer of 1941 he went absent without leave and had to be "apprehended by the civil authority." Presumably he was still prone to the pubbing of his earlier days. His service record shows that he was "severely reprimanded", demoted, and docked two weeks' pay. A little later he regained his rank and was subsequently promoted to Flight Lieutenant. In December 1942 he was posted to North Africa. On February 25, he crashed his jeep in the desert, there was an injury, and he was later diagnosed with an "obsessional psychoneurosis". This was apparently, at the time, an all-purpose term that covered anxiety, depression and so on. Whatever the precise nature of the problem, he was, as his Service Record states, "found below required standard for further service with the R.A.F." and was invalided home.

For the next ten years his life followed a downward trajectory. His separation and divorce from his first wife became final and he married again. It was a marriage that did not last long. He did various jobs including running a pub, driving a taxi and working for a bookie, until the years of hard living took their toll on his health and he became critically ill with tuberculosis. Luckily, a member of the family contributed the money to send him to a sanatorium in Oslo where, after several years he was finally cured. He settled in Norway where he initially earned his living as a teacher and a factory worker. Later, with friends, he established a small publishing company which became the Oslo University Press for which he worked until his retirement to Southampton in 1975. In Oslo he sang in the choir of St. Edmund's cathedral, and it was here that he met his third wife, Sigi, who finally brought stability and peace and happiness into his life. A stroke led to a long spell in hospital where he developed gangrene and his leg was amputated above the knee. He died on December 23rd 1979.

BILL BARAZETTI

It is difficult to know where to begin a biographical note about Barazetti because there are so few verifiable facts about his life, and those few that we have sometimes do not support the colourful stories that have been told about him. In the circumstances it might be appropriate to start at the end of his story, and work backwards.

Bill Barazetti died on September 24th, 2000. An obituary appeared in The Times on October 9th. Seven years earlier, on October 26th 1993, Yad Vashem, the highly respected Holocaust Martyrs and Heroes Remembrance Authority awarded Werner (or Theodore) Barazetti its highest accolade, Righteous Among the Nations, an honour given to those who risked their lives to save Jews during the Holocaust. In 2007 Yad Vashem published its Encyclopedia Of The Righteous. It consists of an article on each person so honoured. From the Times Obituary we learn that Barazetti was "recommended as a partner" in Winton's Kindertransports, and that he "made all the arrangements at the Prague end. He organised the trains, interviewed the families and sent Winton the details and photographs of each child." He then fell foul of the Gestapo, but after a spell in Poland where he got a false passport, he returned to Prague "in disguise" and continued to organise the exit of "664 children". The Yad Vashem Encyclopedia, to some degree probably a source for The Times Obituary, tells much the same story.

Bill Barazetti (1914-2000)
A passport photograph, aged 23

Here we are told that he "saved 669 Jewish children from the clutches of the Nazi oppressors by arranging three transports out of Czechoslovakia for them, mostly to Britain. He was the driving force in the Kindertransport operation, risking his life in this endeavour." And so on and so forth.

Unfortunately the stories in both the Encyclopedia and the Obituary, particularly as they relate to the Kindertransports, are almost completely false. It is difficult to understand how such a tissue of lies came to be written, and why such influential publications as those of Yad Vashem and The Times accepted them as the truth. It may well be that some crucial evidence was not available at the time; it may also be that there was uncritical acceptance of personal narrative.

For our purposes Barazetti's life can conveniently be divided into two parts, the pre-rescue operation years and the months that he actually spent in Prague in 1938/39 helping Doreen Warriner. The latter is the easier to handle because the evidence rests on documented fact, whereas the earlier years are remarkable for their absence of such documentation.

There are four fairly extensive biographical pieces that deal with Barazetti's early life. These are the Yad Vashem Encyclopedia and The Times Obituary, already mentioned, plus an article in the Daily Mail from 1999 and four pages in Vera Gissing's book, *Nicholas Winton and the Rescued Generation*. It is important to note that the information in the Yad Vashem and Times articles is, of course, second-hand; but the latter two were the result of personal interviews and thus may be said to quote Barazetti himself directly, though The Daily Mail article mentions one caveat when trying to sort out the events of Barazetti's life before his Prague days. "The details are clouded in his own mind, confused by the stroke he suffered three years ago." Equally frustrating for the researcher is the absence of documentation. Apparently this was all, according to The Mail, "lost or destroyed in the confusion of a Europe on the brink of total war."

To these four sources can now be added a fifth and a sixth that have recently come to light. The fifth is the Home Office file HO405/3688 that is held at the National Archives at Kew. This file contains information about Barazetti's naturalization application, police reports, court case and so on. The sixth consists of a few documents from the National Archives, Prague.

The four above sources are generally agreed that Barazetti was born on July 29th, 1914 in Switzerland. (though it now appears from the Home Office file that he was born in Hanover of Swiss parents. Or possibly Hamburg.) His father may have been a professor of French at the University of Heidelberg (Obituary) though the university has no record of a Barazetti teaching French at this time, (there is a Cesar Barazetti who taught Economics in the 1880's/90's). All four articles devote space to establishing Barazetti's influential family connections (in Gissing's case this occupies about a quarter of the whole biography), as though these social connections, to a police chief and, more tenuously, to Masaryk, who became President of Czechoslovakia, are in themselves a guarantee of the probity of Barazetti's own character and the accuracy of his adventures. According to all reports he attended Hamburg University in 1933, though the university itself has no record of this. He possibly also went to university in Prague. At Hamburg – if he went there - he studied law (Obituary) or philosophy (Yad Vashem, Daily Mail) or philosophy and economics (Gissing). It was at university that he first saw the mistreatment of Jews and as a result became a lifelong opponent of the Nazis.

If his university career is a bit of a puzzle, it is almost impossible to sort out any coherent sequence of events in the subsequent years up to 1938. Our four sources tell us variously that he joined the Czech Secret Service while at university in Hamburg (The Mail) or in Prague (Yad Vashem). As a spy he was able to discover information at the very highest level. "With my family connections and contacts I was in a unique position to know better than most people what was happening with Hitler and what his plans might be" (The Mail). Gissing agrees that he set out to "try to find out what Hitler's future plans might be." It would, of course, be most useful if we knew a few more details about this espionage in high places, although Gissing does add the intriguing story that he "set up a perfume factory as a cover for his clandestine activities". It would be interesting to know the name of this factory, where it was situated, how many it employed, and so on. One may also note here a fascinating echo of the Schindler story.

Eventually Barazetti's spying was discovered by the Gestapo and depending on the version one reads, he slipped over the Polish border, changed his name, dyed his hair, got a new passport, returned to Germany, was chased again, tried to fake his own death by "leaving his clothes on the banks of the river Elbe to give the impression that he had drowned" (Obituary) or else "by the side of a lake" (The Mail). But eventually the Gestapo caught up with him and he was "taken to a remote forest, beaten and left for dead". It was here, according to most versions, that he met his wife, Anna. "He was discovered on the German-Czech border by a young Czech peasant woman....who dragged him barely alive back to her village home and nursed him back to health" (The

Mail). Gissing agrees: "A young peasant woman found him and nursed him back to health". Yad Vashem changes the romantic scene slightly and Anna becomes "a young Czech girl who helped him recuperate". In the Times Obituary she is quite a different person: "One of his co-workers. . . .was Anna, an idealistic student from the Czech Sudetenland who was at that time sending photographs of Nazi training camps and of the burgeoning rash of labour camps by courier to the press in London". Documents from the Prague National Archives indicate that Anna was born in Hamburg in 1912.

Whether peasant girl or idealistic student, Anna and Barrazetti were married in Prague in 1936. Their first son, Nikolaus, was born in 1937. On top of all these activities, Barazetti also claimed in his naturalization application that he worked for a variety of German, Swiss and Czech newspapers, though when and in what order is unclear (HO405/3688).

But it is now that, with some relief, we can move away from the confusion of memory and anecdotage to a period where we have glimmers of fact. This is not to dismiss these events of the earlier part of Barazetti's life; only to acknowledge that they are almost impossible to grapple with when there is so little in the way of objective proof of these events. If it is true that for the historian there can be no authentication without verification then the Barazetti story between 1933 and 1938 has to be treated with the utmost caution. The Prague archives give us very broad proof of his movements from 1936. In that year he had to leave Germany because of his anti-Nazi beliefs, and came to Czechoslovakia as a stateless person who was hoping to study at the university of Prague (sign B 370/89). He had a temporary Czech passport. In 1937, he applied for and received a six month visa to go to Switzerland where he hoped to find work. In Switzerland he applied for citizenship but was turned down. He and his wife arrived back in Prague early in 1938. He also tried to emigrate to Sweden. It is also at this time that he possibly tried to become a police informer. He went to an Intelligence Office to report someone for being a suspected Nazi spy. He was not, however, involved in the subsequent investigation, and a note on the report says that Barazetti himself was considered unreliable (sign 200-254-40;202-37-14). Life must have been very hard for him at this time. As a German trying to exist in Prague on a temporary passport, a refugee amongst thousands of other refugees, it must have been a matter of doing whatever was necessary to put bread on the table for himself and his family.

It is impossible to say when Barazetti started to work for Warriner - though it was probably a little before Christmas 1938 - or how he came to do so. It is just possible that he was working for the Czech Red Cross (HO405/3688), and subsequently transferred his services to the BCRC. As one of the hordes of refugees in Prague at the time (his BCRC refugee number was 5817) he must have introduced himself to her, and demonstrated that he was a useful worker who could take care of some of the typing and filing, and more importantly, could speak German and Czech fluently. This would have been invaluable to Warriner. No doubt he made the work of handing out the appropriate forms and answering questions that much easier. A later letter will support and expand on this.

Thus Barazetti makes his first documented appearance in our Kindertransport story in a letter that Winton wrote, possibly to his mother, around January 7th/8th, 1939. As we have seen, Winton's most important contact in Prague was Doreen Warriner, and her refugee office on Vorsilska St was probably the centre of his own activities. On the occasion of this first letter he is still new enough to the situation to get names wrong. He writes: "All the people who want to see Miss Warriner for information or help are asked to go any or every day to Vorsilska 2. There they are met by Barbazetti (sic) (and today me as well) and they are dealt with." Elsewhere in the letter he calls Barazetti "the secretary of Miss Warriner."

The next reference is in a letter of Winton's dated January 11th to his friend Martin Blake. "Well Miss Warriner and I are busy compiling lists and getting things ready for the big push. All the children's committees will be coordinated here, very likely under Barbazetti (sic), but he does not know it yet." Worth noting is the fact that when the all important refugee "Lists" are being compiled it is done by Warriner and Winton. Barazetti is not included in the discussions because, as a refugee himself, it would have been inappropriate for him to be involved with matters of eligibility and priority. As Warriner wrote in a letter (see page 98), "he [Barazetti] never deals with Lists or recommendations." It is also interesting that when Warriner and Winton discussed, as they must have done, what was to happen when Winton (and Chadwick) returned to London, as they did a week later, it was assumed that Barazetti, though he wasn't consulted, could "hold the fort", presumably because it was seen as another job that could be done out of Warriner's office.

Two days after Winton left Prague, Warriner sent Margaret Layton, the Honorary Secretary of the BCRC back in London a short note with a few names that Warriner wanted added to the official refugee Lists. It reads, "I want to submit again the following names". Three of the names are those of Barazetti and his wife and child. This tells us that though he had found some form of employment in the Warriner offices, he, like tens of thousands of others, is eager to become a part of the emigration process, the first step of which was to get registered on the all important Lists. This is also the only time that Anna and Nikolaus are mentioned in these earlier documents.

Back in London, Winton now had to start the complex task of getting his children's transports off the ground. This entailed writing a large number of letters and statements and manifestos and press releases and circulars to all and sundry explaining what he was trying to do, and pleading for support and money. As was explained earlier, in these early days Winton's operation had no status, no money, no office, and wasn't even recognized by the BCRC. He had to create his operation from the ground up. One of these documents, probably written sometime in February, or soon after he got back to London, contains the statement that has caused so much confusion and misunderstanding as regards Barazetti's contribution to the Kindertransport project. It reads,

> *I have recently returned from 3 weeks in Prague during which time I co-ordinated all the Children's Committees under one head. Mr. Barazetti, who is Miss Warriner's secretary, is now also the responsible official for all children in Czechoslovakia, who wish to come to England.*

In what is probably a different manifesto to another audience Winton writes:

> *I have brought back with me about 500 case papers with photographs of these children, covering all the Czechoslovakian Committees, and am in continual touch*

with Mr. Barazetti in Prague so that no overlapping can occur in the event of children being sent from Czechoslovakia to other countries.

It is easy to see how these quotations, particularly the first one, have misled people, particularly those unwilling to look at all the evidence, into maintaining that Barazetti was responsible for the Prague Kindertransports. One may note first of all that both of these pieces are what could be called propaganda in the sense that Winton's object in writing them was to impress possible sponsors, guarantors, financial contributors, etc., that the children's rescue operation that he was trying to set up was a worthy cause, that its foundations were well established and that it was being efficiently run. In fact Winton was having considerable difficulty being accepted by the BCRC, which, as we know, was more concerned with the adult refugees. It is significant too that in the first excerpt we are told that Barazetti is *"also"* to be the responsible official for the children. The "also" is important. It can only mean that it is expected that he will continue to work for Warriner, but that he will "also" be keeping an eye on Winton's newly started children's project. Though Winton and Chadwick were away, no doubt there was still much filing and organizing of documentation, and handing out forms, and passing on information about children who should no longer be on Lists, and so on. This would almost certainly have remained under the overall supervision of Warriner.

But the more important proof, of course, that this was a temporary job for Barazetti lies in the fact that, as has been well documented, Chadwick came out to run the Prague end of the Kindertransports at the end of February. There is a huge weight of evidence, as we have seen, that this was so, and perhaps it would not be amiss to repeat the passage from Winton's letter quoted on p. 72, describing how the Kindertransports were organized. "Trevor came out and offered his help and we set up an office together and he agreed to run the Czech side....[He] then went to work and dealt with all the considerable problems at the Prague end and this work he continued to carry on even when it became difficult and dangerous when the Germans arrived. He deserves all praise." (On March 17, 2010, during a talk to Sevenoaks School school about the Kindertransports, Winton said, "of course none of this (the Kindertransports) would have been possible without Trevor Chadwick.")

It is a pity that Winton's letter was not available to the researchers for the Yad Vashem Encyclopedia article and the Times obituary, though it is worth noting that documents such as Warriner's and Stopford's memoirs were already in the public domain. Warriner's "A Winter in Prague" in particular has ample evidence about who ran the Prague office, but this was ignored. And it is easy to see how the misunderstandings began and grew. For example, if one were to ask, "Did Barazetti help with the saving of the Prague refugee children?" the answer would be, "Yes, he certainly did. The work he did in Warriner's office, particularly with his language skills, while the project was being launched was very useful." But that this should become inflated into the claim that "he was the driving force in the Kindertransport operation, risking his life in this endeavour" is clearly untrue. How untrue will become even clearer later.

The next reference to Barazetti comes in a very long letter about him that Warriner wrote to Layton on February 22nd,

1939. The letter is important enough to quote in full.

Dear Miss Layton

With reference to Barazetti himself I am anxious to keep him here as long as possible because he is so very useful; he takes off an endless amount of detailed work from me and I have found him always sympathetic and kind to the refugees. Garratt may have told you that there are doubts
about the advisability of employing a refugee in such a confidential position, and there was a time about three weeks ago when he was interviewed by the police when I doubted it myself. But he is to my mind entirely trustworthy, and I feel I can better judge this than the other refugees; his character seems to me a very sound one (with the usual German defect of feeling too much about injustice) and he is extremely intelligent. Also it is often a relief to me to have someone of very similar tastes and interests (he was an economist) to discuss things with. When he came to me he was in a really desperate state but never said so and for a long time he continued to do odd jobs of typing until I decided he could easily take over the full time job. He never deals with lists or recommendations and has also no axe to grind.... I'm 'very pleased with him for having organized a group of 30 children to Sweden, entirely on his own with Winton's help. I do not want to keep him indefinitely (Warriner's emphasis) for his own sake, since the work leads nowhere but it is obviously better for him to stay here, than to come over to England, where he cannot do much, for the time being. Garratt I think proposes to ask you to find me a secretary, but I do not think the Committee will want to contemplate a big expense like this, and I feel I ought to explain to you that I should like to help him at least for a few more weeks, unless the situation grows worse, in which case he'd have to go.
Yours sincerely
Doreen Warriner

The first thing to notice about this letter is that it was written over a month after Winton's visit and suggests that Warriner was rather slow about getting clearance from Margaret Layton, her boss in London, for Barazetti to work for her. It is impossible to say why this was so. Perhaps she was eager to retain him as her "secretary" because she enjoyed his manner and intelligence, and preferred him to the unknown official secretary that was being suggested for her. Her admiration for his work was unbounded and she even, and rather amusingly, over-eggs the praise when she mentions the plane load of children to Sweden (presumably this was the one that involved the beautiful Swedish spy mentioned in the Warriner chapter) that he organized "*entirely* on his own" (her emphasis), but then rather spoils the effect by adding "with Winton's help" . It is interesting that when Winton describes this plane transport he says that he himself put it together and doesn't mention any contribution of Barazetti's.

Intriguing too is the interview with the Czech police mentioned in the letter particularly in light of Barazetti's claim that he worked for them in Germany, but since there is no further information about the subject of this interview we are reduced to empty speculation. Gissing makes the interesting suggestion that his main job in the refugee world was to keep an eye out for Nazi spies who might try to smuggle themselves aboard the transports as a way of getting to England.
As she says,

> *His main job originally was to smooth the way with government administration and to ensure that no Nazi spies had a free passage to England when groups of refugees and other enemies of the Reich began to leave... ."I used to know most of them", Barazetti told me. "Big*

*Nazis, small crooks and their innocent victims." He
continued to work under the assumed name of Le Monnier
because he was afraid of endangering the rescue operation
if his past anti-Nazi activities came to light.*

There is, of course, no proof of this counter-espionage role,
though there is ample evidence that he worked in Warriner's
office at fairly mundane tasks. On the other hand, if he was
involved in some form of undercover work one wonders
whether Warriner knew about it and would have approved.
Her later letters suggest that she didn't know and would not
have approved. (The suggestion that he worked under the
name of Le Monnier at this time makes little sense. Everyone
referred to him by his real name, which would anyway have
been on his temporary Czech passport.)

More significant is Warriner's sensitivity about the
propriety of hiring a refugee. Clearly she is aware of the
unwritten rule that in the sometimes delicate business in which
she was involved it was unacceptable for refugees to be put in
charge of other refugees, and she expresses her own doubts
about the advisability of "employing a refugee in such a
confidential position", but makes it clear that she knows where
the boundaries lie. "He never deals with lists or
recommendations."

But on the whole the letter is a glowing tribute to Barazetti's
qualities, and an expression of pleasure that she can work
with someone who apparently "speaks her language". Within
a month she had changed her mind quite radically.

Barazetti next appears on March 15th, 1939, the day that the
German army marched into Prague. As may be imagined, the
day was pure chaos throughout the city, and the British
Legation, where Warriner had temporarily set up an office,

was no exception. Warriner has a moving description of the desperation and the confusion of that day in her memoir:

The stairs were thronged with refugees, all desperate...
Luckily the day before I had remembered to take the
balance of the News Chronicle Fund, about £5000, out of
the bank, so I gave them money and told those I knew to
make a dash for the frontier and get to the British
Consulate in Katowice. If they were on the old visa lists,
I gave them a signed visiting card with a note to the
Consul to this effect.... I collected all the passports in my
desk - they belonged to the Sudeten communists – and
called to the crowd in the passage and on the stairs that
they must get away, because the Gestapo would come at
any moment. Then I went back to the hotels where several
terrified refugees came up to me....A call from London
came through and I took it in the box in the hall; it was
Miss Rathbone, to say that anyone I recommended for a
visa would get one. The German General Staff were milling
round the box - they were being quartered in the Alcron -
so I felt the decision was too late. I left Margaret Dougan
destroying all the papers in our rooms, and took a taxi to
the Legation, with the box of passports....

Stopford described the same day almost as vividly in his diary so we have two perspectives on the events. And it is Stopford who gives us our next sighting of Barazetti. He explained in his diary that the Legation decided to offer asylum to "a small number of people who were in great danger and who had some special claim on us." There are eight of them, and Stopford divides them into three categories. Category (i) consists of Sudeten Social Democrats. They included Jaksch and Taub, the two leaders of the Social Democrats. (Jaksch knew that the Germans would eventually demand his surrender, so he slipped out of the embassy in disguise as a workman and was smuggled across the Polish border.) Category (ii) was Katz, a communist, and Stopford appends a seventeen line footnote to explain his presence. Category (iii) also consists of one name. "Herr Barazetti a member of Miss Warriner's Secretariat." The inclusion of Barazetti poses many problems. The reason why the first two categories were offered asylum is self evident. As leading anti-Nazis they were "marked men". But no reason is given for Barazetti's inclusion. Once again there are several possibilities. Was he, after all, an undercover agent for Czech intelligence as he claimed? Had his exploits in Germany and elsewhere a few years earlier caught up with him once again? Were the Gestapo after him because of his anti-Nazi views – and there is no reason to believe that these were not genuine. Or was it Warriner who was trying to assist a man who had been a loyal employee? It is almost impossible to answer these questions, and they are made even more complicated by other data that surfaced shortly afterwards.

Meanwhile, it is important to note the dates. Barazetti took asylum in the British Legation on March 15th. On March 20th the Germans were given the names of the eight refugees in the Legation. On March 24th the Germans said "the men would receive safe-conducts provided that they had not been charged with High Treason, espionage or a political offence involving the use of explosives." On March 28th the Germans declared that all these refugees (except Jaksch) were free to go, and asked for their passports. The passports were surrendered and returned two days later with their exit permits. Stopford then shepherded the little party to safety: "I saw the party off on the night train on 1st April, in case any tricks were tried at the station, and breathed a sigh of relief when we heard that they were finally across the frontier". What are we to make of the Gestapo's apparent indifference to Barazetti's identity? Does this cast a shadow on the internal efficiency of the Gestapo intelligence machine? Or does it cast more of a shadow on the veracity of Barazetti's stories about his earlier exploits?

In the final analysis it doesn't really matter which of these options we choose to pursue. The crucial piece of factual evidence that we have are the dates. Barazetti took asylum in the British Legation on March 15th and eventually left for England on April 1st. (His wife and son had left for England three days before the Germans arrived, probably on one of Warriner's transports.) He went by train to Poland, and then flew to Croydon where he landed on April 7th. If we compare these dates with those of the Kindertransports on the following page, we can see that he could have had very little to do with them for the simple reason that he wasn't in Prague. In short, to claim that he was "the driving force in the Kindertransport operation" (Yad Vashem) or that he "played a major part in organizing the escape of children from German-occupied Prague" (Times Obituary) can't be true.

We can also note that both of these articles state that Barazetti was responsible for "saving" 669 children (664 in the Obituary), and if we look once again at the official list of the Kindertransports we can see where these numbers come from. It is, of course, the *total* number of children who were put on the transports. What is amusing is that both articles say Barazetti should have credit only for three transports, presumably those in June, July and August (when he was in England) but fail in their arithmetic when they quote the total for all eight transports.

A final letter that we should quote from gives us proof that

MOVEMENT FOR THE CARE OF CHILDREN FROM GERMANY, Ltd.
BRITISH INTER-AID COMMITTEE

Room 61,
BLOOMSBURY HOUSE,
BLOOMSBURY STREET,
LONDON, W.C.1.

Telephone : MUSeum 2900 Ext. 61.

CZECH SECTION

Report 'B' – 2nd October 1939

STATEMENT OF CHILDREN BROUGHT OVER UP TO THE 1ST SEPTEMBER 1939
SHOWING OUR COMMITMENTS FOR RE-EMIGRATION GUARANTEES

Transports from Prague:

1st	14th March 1939	20
2nd	19th April 1939	36
3rd	29th April 1939	29
4th	13th May 1939	61
5th	2nd June 1939	123
6th	1st July 1939	241
7th	20th July 1939	76
8th	2nd August 1939	68
Various transports from Vienna, etc.		15
	Total	669

Specification of obligations:

Before re-emigration deposit required			20
of which –	Boys under 12	5	
	Girls under 12	13	
	Girls over 12	2	

Re-emigration deposits, etc.:

Cheques and cash deposits	83	
Securities	1	
Bank guarantees	50	
Personal guarantees	134	
Other Committees	116	
Movement	28	
Czech Trust Fund	22	
Children's Section	177	591
Children who travelled on own visum		58
Total		669

Barazetti reached London safely. It also supplies a possible reason for why he left. The letter is from Warriner to Margaret Layton at the BCRC headquarters in London. It is a reply to the latter's earlier letter asking Warriner for advice about what she should do with Barazetti who had turned up at her office. She writes:

> *I understand Barazetti is doing some refugee work; I think it would be better to relieve him of any duties in connection with it as he is now in a very unbalanced state of mind and though he is a very competent worker he cannot be given responsibility in a difficult situation. I am afraid that unless he gets entirely away from the refugee situation his character will suffer. Paul Yates can find him sedative employment doing economic research.* (HO 294/53)

Once again we are left in the realms of speculation as we try to guess what lay behind Warriner's remarkable about-face. In little more than a month he has changed from being her blue-eyed boy to a serious liability. Indeed , one wonders whether the reason for his inclusion in the Legation's asylum group lies somewhere beneath these lines. Was he perhaps having a breakdown, and did Warriner feel an obligation to him because of his past services and so helped him to leave Prague? It is even difficult to decide whether the tone of her comments is censorious or sympathetic.

Warriner makes one further reference in London to Barazetti four months later in a diary entry. On August 17th she writes, "Awful morning dealing with Barazetti. Miss Bracey went with me." Not much, of course, can be concluded from this cryptic comment. It appears that she felt she still had obligations towards Barazetti, (when the family first arrived in London she allowed them to stay in her flat in Belsize Park) but now takes no pleasure at all in his company. She takes a friend with her, perhaps as witness, perhaps for moral support. It is also proof that he was living in England at this time.

The Prague archival material (sign2-90/380) gives us a strong hint as to why Warriner's relationship with Barazetti ended, and also maybe accounts for her "awful morning dealing with Barazetti" mentioned above, and why when she came to write her memoir, *A Winter in Prague*, some years later, a memoir filled with names and dates and detail, she never once mentions the name of Barazetti her former "secretary".

At some point in 1940/41 Barazetti wrote a letter to the President's Office of the Czech Government in Exile accusing Warriner and Jaksch, who we remember was the leader of the Sudetenland refugees, also now in exile, of spreading rumours about him and blackening his reputation. The letter is a sort of pre-emptive strike by Barazetti against the other two, and he gives a longish list of the great and the good, inevitably including Masaryk himself, who will testify to his moral probity. The letter has a handwritten note on it, presumably written by some Czech official, stating that the BCRC will no longer vouch for Barazetti as he has been involved in financial fraud. Another letter, this one from the exiled Ministry of the Interior, advises the President's Office that this is a personal matter between Warriner and Barazetti, that it should be dealt with by an English court, and that anyway Barazetti isn't a Czech national.

What this case was all about must remain a matter of guesswork, but it is possible that what happened was that some refugees found that when they got to London some of their possessions, or valuables of various sorts, had disappeared, or that they were victims of some sort of financial deception. They went to their leader, Jaksch, and complained, and he immediately took it up with Warriner. If there is any truth in this suggestion, then it would certainly be reason enough for Warriner having nothing more to do with her former "secretary". However, it should be emphasized that this is all speculative. The matter seems to have come before an Aliens' Tribunal, but we do not how it was resolved. What is certain is that the charge of fraud stuck to Barazetti for a long time. It was part of the evidence during his later trial for theft and during his citizenship hearings.

But we must also consider whether it is remotely possible that Barazetti, having arrived in England with his family in April, slipped *back* to Prague at some later date and was responsible for the June, July and August transports as the Times Obituary and the Yad Vashem Encyclopedia state. Such a suggestion is far-fetched in the extreme. To begin with we must remember that the Children's Section office in Prague had been running smoothly for some time. When Walter Creighton arrived some time early in June to take over the refugee work from Stopford, he immediately advised that the BCRC office be closed down at least temporarily, but on July 8th writes to London that "The Jewish children's work must anyhow continue. We have great obligations there and it is a wonderful work." Whatever system Chadwick had put in place, it seemed to be functioning efficiently, and the Gestapo were continuing to sign the exit permits with few objections. But we also need to imagine this Kindertransport office on Rubesova St. It was obviously filled with masses of files and documents and forms and telegrams and letters, and the general paraphernalia that one would associate with such a large rescue operation, all being processed by its secretarial help. Through June the largest transport was taking shape satisfactorily. Is it in any way conceivable that in this situation Barazetti would walk in one day and announce that he would be taking over the transports? Two months earlier he had been considered to be in a "very unbalanced state of mind" and unfit to deal with refugees. In such circumstances would the BCRC have sanctioned such a takeover? And is it possible that they would have abandoned their previous policy of not using refugees to run the affairs of other refugees? And if Barazetti had somehow got involved wouldn't his name have appeared somewhere in the minutes of BCRC meetings, or possibly in someone's letter? To analyse the practicalities of the suggestion is to highlight its impossibility.

And what anyway are we to make of the Encyclopedia and the Obituary assertions that Barazetti undertook his rescue work in disguise, with a false identity and that he forged the exit visas for the refugees? As the Encyclopedia puts it, "Although a wanted man and working under an assumed name he succeeded in persuading the German authorities in Prague to send three rail transports of children to Britain". What must puzzle us is why he was considered a wanted man when he had earlier been cleared by the Gestapo and given a safe conduct to England? And why, too, did he think he needed to change his name and disguise himself. He was known as Barazetti by Warriner, Stopford, and Winton, and as Warriner's major domo through the early months of 1939 he must have become a well known figure in Prague both in the refugee community and to the authorities. And one would certainly like more detail about how he managed the considerable feat of negotiating transports and documents with the Gestapo while "a wanted man" with a fake identity. Surely the Gestapo were not that slow-witted! In conclusion it is hard not to attribute the bulk of these stories to an over-active imagination rather than to fact.

But to these practical considerations we may now add the evidence contained in the aforementioned files (HO405/3688) newly made available at the National Archives. Most of the files pertaining to Barazetti contain documents relating to his two applications for naturalization. The first application was in 1947, two years after he finished his work with M.I. 19. However, this was turned down mainly because he was convicted of theft and receiving in a Bedfordshire court, and sentenced to 12 months imprisonment, reduced to eight months on appeal. He made a second attempt to get naturalization in 1956. In Part 7 of the application form he enters, as required, the details of his criminal record, but he adds the note, in capital letters, "Convicted on the strength of witness of a convicted criminal – I was innocent though foolish not to engage a solicitor."

At this second attempt the initial evaluations were not positive, but there were also some sympathetic, but rather double-edged, assessments The assessor wrote:

I am not convinced that the refusal of these applications, first made in 1946, should be, maintained . It is true that in 1939 there were strong grounds for suspicion that he was using his position with the BCRC to his financial benefit at the expense of some of the refugees but it must be remembered that he was only 25 at the time and the opportunities for easy money from people who were desperately anxious to get away from Nazi control offered strong temptations. It is also true that he was sentenced

in 1947 for being concerned in stealing and receiving – an
indication that his moral standards were little better at
33 than they were at 25. On the credit side however.... the
impression I get from the police reports is of a man who
has tried – with some success - to rehabilitate himself....

The references to cheating the other refugees, mentioned in two or three of the accounts, plus reports about smuggling jewelry or something similar, have been mentioned earlier. More significant for our purposes is the statement on the forms that were sent to the Home Office from the Bedford Police that "since arriving in this country in 1939, he has not visited any other foreign country". On top of all the other evidence adduced above, we can add that it is unlikely that he would tell a lie on this crucial application, his second attempt to acquire U.K. citizenship, and that, in other words, this is further proof that Barazetti did not leave England after he arrived on April 7th, 1939, and therefore had very little to do with the Prague Kindertransports.

One further fact can, I think, finish the argument. When making his two applications for citizenship it was important that he present himself in the most favourable light possible. On both occasions, his work for MI. 19 was noted and this, as is stated, swayed the assessors. On the first occasion, of course, the jail term discounted this advantage, but when he re-applied ten years later his wartime service was a real factor in the success of the application. But nowhere in either application is there any mention whatsoever that he had saved the lives of 669 children from the Nazis. This omission is all the more remarkable when we remember that the horrors of the Holocaust were still relatively recent. Maybe one reason why he did not mention it is because Warriner, Wellington and Chadwick were all still alive, and might have queried the claim that he was "the driving force in the Kindertransport operation".

Finally we may come back to the question of how it happened that two highly respected publications such as The Times and the Yad Vashem Encyclopedia came to promote a story that is so full of falsifications. It is important because both are publications of record; what they publish becomes etched in stone in the public's mind and will be turned to in years to come as repositories of the Truth. In Barazetti's case it appears to have been a chance remark at a conference in 1989 that set the ball rolling. One day the Kindertransports were mentioned, and "Barazetti said he knew something about that, since he had had some slight involvement with the transport of children from Prague." (Obituary) Ironically, if the story had been left at that it would have been perfectly true. As we have seen, as Warriner's "secretary" he did indeed play a (very small) part.

Coincidentally we may remember that it was just the year before, 1988, that the Winton story had burst on the world with the articles in The Sunday Mirror and Esther Rantzen's That's Life television show. This was followed by Winton being feted in Jerusalem, where his diaries and papers were deposited in the Winton Archives, and subsequently becoming a celebrity in many other countries. And it is now that Barazetti was also vigorously promoted as another unsung hero of the Prague Kindertransports of fifty years earlier, and this enthusiastic and imaginative advocacy culminated in his being awarded Yad Vashem's honour of Righteous Among the Nations in 1993. And by now Chadwick, Warriner and Wellington had all been dead for ten or fifteen years and were unable to comment.

It is, of course, most regrettable that Yad Vashem did not

have access to some of the more recent evidence in this case, though it must be repeated that Warriner's *A Winter in Prague*, for example, was available for consultation, and should in itself have set alarm bells ringing. Instead, there seems to have been too easy a reliance on uncorroborated reminiscences, an absence of a critical approach to evidence, and perhaps a misplaced, though understandable, enthusiasm for someone mistakenly thought to have saved many lives. And then, one imagines, the point was reached by those promoting the Barazetti case when so much time, energy and emotion had been invested that it was difficult to turn back. Even when later evidence surfaced that cast serious and conclusive doubts on Barazetti's story, the difficulty of admitting there had been a mistake was probably too powerful, and it was easier to go on than to go back.

Yad Vashem itself was extremely polite when these matters were brought to its attention, but of course was in a difficult position. It was clearly impossible to change or remove the Encyclopedia entry, and apparently there is no mechanism to deprive the false claimant of his title. This is a pity simply because some might wonder about the integrity of the Encyclopedia. If such egregious mistakes can slip through, how many other errors or exaggerations might there be? But these are issues for Yad Vashem to resolve. Sadly, this particular fabrication remains enshrined in two otherwise respected reference works.

As an addendum, I should mention that Yad Vashem's final comment, after they had seen this present chapter with all its factual evidence was,

> *I understand your concern with what was written in the*
> *Encyclopedia of the Righteous, but I can only reiterate*
> *that the Encyclopedia's purpose is not intended to depict*
> *the Kindertransport activity in its entirety, but merely*

*provides the stories of those who were awarded the title
of Righteous Among the Nations by Yad Vashem.*

It is perhaps surprising that Yad Vasehm is not concerned
about whether the stories it publishes are true or false, but
there I think we must leave this matter.

* * *

In May, 1940, Barazetti was interned as an alien, but a year
later his language skills got him released. He worked for M.I.
19 the Intelligence department responsible for interrogating
German prisoners of war. He was employed at the Beaconsfield
branch probably as a translator until September 1, 1945. After
his jail term in 1947, he worked in a printer's office in St.
Albans for ten years. He became a British citizen in 1957, and
may have worked for the United Nations. For many years he
was the Assistant Treasurer, and then became the Hon.
Treasurer of P.E.N from 1991 - 1996. In his later years he fell on
hard times. The story of his plight reached an Israeli newspaper
where it came to the notice of Hugo Marom. Himself a Prague
child refugee, he wrote to some 200 other former refugees and
asked them to contribute to a fund to help the man who, it was
thought, had saved their lives. The response was generous
and Barazetti was able to pay off his debts and also receive an
income of £ 500 a month. He died on September 24th, 2000.

BEATRICE WELLINGTON

Beatrice Wellington's childhood was convoluted. She was born on June 15, 1907, and her father, whose name was Gonzales, left the family soon afterwards. She appeared to be the youngest of five siblings, four girls and a boy, though she discovered when she was about twelve that they were actually three aunts, one uncle and one mother. Relationships had been camouflaged in order to make life smoother. Her ex-sibling mother, Lily, married George Wellington. He was an oppressive step-father much resented by his intelligent, independent-minded daughter. There were many arguments in the family. For example, against her wishes, he insisted that she take his name. When she first went to Europe he insisted on registering her for her first passport, and as a result it announced her as Wellington, and that is the name she was known by throughout her time in Europe. This was to have tragic repercussions later on. In her last years, when she was teaching in Edmonton, Alberta, and elsewhere, she became Gonzales once again.

Lily and George eventually had a child together, William, a half-brother with whom Beatrice created a strong bond of affection. It is perhaps from this discordant childhood that she developed a sense of defiance, a hatred of injustice and a strong streak of anti-authoritarianism that for better or for worse were to mark her life.

Like Warriner, Wellington was academically a high achiever. She went to the University of British Columbia, one of the first women to do so, when she was 17 and graduated three years later in 1927 with a major in English and History.

Beatrice Wellington (1907 – 1971)

Her Dean of Women commented on her "exceptional ability and brilliance in her studies". From university she immediately became a teacher, first at Point Grey Junior High School (1928-31) and then at Chilliwack High School (1931-36). During these years she had developed an interest in European politics in general, and the League of Nations in particular, and no doubt as the European pot began to boil in the second half of the 1930's she felt that Chilliwack was a bit remote from the events unfolding across the Atlantic. She took a one year leave of absence from her teaching and went to take a closer look at what appeared to be a developing crisis.

She started off in Geneva, though in what capacity is hard to pin down. One report states that it was Canadian Quakers who sent her there; another states that she was "assistant secretary to an American woman who was in charge of a youth group movement" in Geneva; a third that she went "to a Youth Congress and later found work in the bureau of employment for women in the International Labour Office (I.L.O.)". She was also in Austria, (probably Vienna) in 1938 when Hitler marched in. It is quite possible that these apparently different jobs are connected in some way, though how they all fit together is not clear. It is equally possible that Wellington picked up employment as and when she could, rather like the modern student on a "gap year". Certainly one can already detect one aspect of her personality that was to be dominant in her life. She was an absolute mistress of what today we would call networking. She was fazed by no one and by nothing. When she wanted something, whether it was information, or explanations, or precious documents, or assistance, she invariably went straight to the source of the problem, probably without waiting for an appointment.

"Hesitation" is not a word that one associates with her.

In 1938, a Vancouver newspaper reported that "she was appointed to take charge of a Y.W.C.A summer camp in Czechoslovakia", and this must have been when she saw the dreadful refugee problem at first hand. When the camp concluded and she had taken the girls back to Geneva, she returned to Prague. Like Warriner and Winton and Chadwick, she wanted to do something to help. Thirty years after these events, Dr. Wellington, her half-brother, wrote an account of these European ventures of his older sister:

> *Although holding a British passport as a Canadian, she was not an embassy official. Although she did not have full diplomatic immunity, she was in a quasi-official capacity as a field officer of an international organization [I.L.O.? Y.W.C.A.?]. Thus she was able to move through official circles more freely than embassy staff or Czech government officials and far more freely than any private citizen....By various means which are still not clear, she began to provide the most endangered refugees with whom she had contact, with new identities drawn from the 'business visa' files of the embassies of safe countries... mainly Britain. Holding visas that allowed business trips out of Czechoslovakia enabled many of those people to escape with their families to the West. And I doubt that anyone knows to this day just how many hundreds of individuals she helped escape in that way.*

As Wellington says, the precise modus operandi that his sister employed to, for example, extract "new identities" drawn from the "business files" of the [British] embassy is very far from clear, but that she seems to have been able to procure necessary documents where others had failed seems to be born out by the case history of the Munk family. Their story was conveyed to the writer by Michael Munk by E-mail.

Frank and Nadia were comfortably off. They lived in a large house on a hill overlooking Prague with their two children, Michael and Suzanne. They had a maid and a cook. Frank was Jewish; Nadia was not. They were, of course, extremely conscious of the increasing anti-semitism, and witnessed the German occupation of the Sudetenland and then of Czechoslovakia itself with mounting horror. But they were loathe to leave their house and their friends and the city they loved, and surely the Nazi foolishness would blow over in time, or would be brought to a halt by saner heads. It was the classic mindset of so many Jewish families at that time. And then it was too late.

Nadia had been doing refugee relief work through 1938, and had met Beatrice Wellington who had warned her that she and her husband were in serious danger. They got confirmation of this on the day that the German army marched into Prague when

> *A stranger visited Frank's business office. He showed Frank a card which identified the visitor as an officer in the former Czech Secret Service. The Visitor said, "I am to show you a little paper. I am sure you will not need an explanation." It was a Gestapo order to arrest all members of the Economic Committee of the National Socialist Party. Frank said, "My name was on top since I served as its chairman. I thanked him and went home directly to tell Nadia – "We do have to get out as soon as possible." Frank never knew who sent this mysterious messenger, and he never saw the man again.*

Unfortunately, when the Munks began to get their documents together they found that the Gestapo turned down their application for an exit visa, the Ausreise. They tried to buy forged documents through illegal channels, but the Gestapo got to the forger before they did. It was at this point that Wellington (who Frank Munk later described as "a person of great courage and extraordinary vision and cleverness") contacted them to see if they had taken her advice about leaving. They explained how they had tried desperately to get the necessary documents but without success. A couple of days later, Munk tells us, Wellington came round to their house with the four grey exit visas, all signed by the Gestapo.

What sleight of hand Wellington used to get the Munks out of the country is not absolutely clear. She had at the time been arranging, quite legally, a train transport for some of the wives and children of men who had previously emigrated to Britain. What she appears to have done is add four extra children to the sanctioned list. Frank became 6 years old, and Nadia 5. Then somehow, when these names were transposed to the forms, only the passport numbers and names were given; the ages were omitted. They left on May 20. This must have been one of Warriner's transports as the date doesn't correspond with any of the Chadwick Kindertransports. Wellington saw them off at the Wilson station. Apparently she had helped a number of other people to escape in this way. As she told Nadia: "Whenever she saw people off at the station, her knees were like boiled macaroni."

The whole journey was nerve-wracking for the Munks. Thirty minutes after leaving Wilson station, the train reached the German border.

The Munks were virtually the only passengers in their railroad car; the refugee children were in the other cars. When the train stopped at the border, two SS men in black uniforms with skull and cross bones on their hats, members of the S.S. Death Head Brigade, asked for documents.

Frank wrote: "My spirits sank to the lowest level ever. I turned over our passports, our Gestapo permits, and also our tickets. [One man asked] "How did you get the exit permit? I knew we would be lost if I seemed worried. I answered very businesslike, "If you have any questions why don't you call your headquarters in Prague and they will tell you."The S.S. officer noted that there were no ages on the cards, just names and passport numbers. They said nothing, collected the documents and walked straight to the station building. [Had the S.S. officers phoned Prague, the ages on file there would have exposed the entire scheme] but before reaching the station they turned in their tracks and came back to the train. Frank was prepared to be arrested, but instead they simply said, "Heil Hitler. We wish you a pleasant trip".

It only became a pleasant trip when they finally reached the Dutch border. From here they took the ferry across to Harwich and so to London. A short time later the Munk family were on a steamship to the United States where Frank became a professor of economics at Reed College in Portland, Oregon. A short time later he took a short trip up to Vancouver in British Columbia, Canada where he gave an address to the Vancouver Institute. The report of his speech in the local press is rich in the hyperbole of gratitude, but this is understandable:

You in Vancouver must be proud of Miss Wellington. She was known the length and breadth of my little country as "Bea"....From the time of Munich to the real war itself [she] was the only person who could give effective help to the "dangerous" refugee cases. Czech democrats, political leaders, Jews, Catholics and Socialists today bless her name in a dozen countries.

Wellington first appears on the BCRC radar on January 21, 1939 where she is mentioned at a committee meeting. The minute reads: "Is Miss Wellington actually representing the Int. Centre for Aid to Prague or is she there on her own?" In other words, "Who is this lady, and who is she working for?" At the beginning of March her opinions about who should be considered a "refugee" are being discussed at a BCRC meeting back in London which suggests not only that she is working closely with their rescue operations, but also that her opinions are worthy of consideration. She had become a figure of authority. But if she was already beginning to interact with the BCRC, at the same time she appears to have continued what we might call her private, free-lance work, and had an office at the Czech Refugee Institute, the official Czech organization that dealt with Jewish emigration. From one brief comment it appears that she may have specialized in procuring visas for those who would emigrate in order to become maids, or home help of some sort.

She makes her first appearance in Warriner's memoir, *A Winter in Prague*, on April 14th. By then the Germans had been in the city for a month, and the Gestapo's influence was beginning to infiltrate the rescue work of the aid agencies. That morning the Gestapo appeared at Wellington's hostel. It is thought they were looking for Margaret Dougan and Christine Maxwell, Warriner's two chief assistants in the illegal emigration scheme, but they were not in so they took Wellington instead who, as it happens, had not been party to these illegalities. In Warriner's account,

> *They took [her] to their office on Perstyn, probably thinking that they had got me; in appearance we were rather alike. They did the usual third degree questioning – questions repeated, then answered before she could speak, all bearing on the English refugee workers.*

Wellington's detention must have been something of a reality check for the aid workers. That same evening, Maxwell and Dougan were bundled quietly onto a train out of Czechoslovakia by the consulate, who didn't want their diplomatic work cluttered with embarrassing arrests due to smuggling activities. Stopford also describes these events:

> *On the 14th the Gestapo had visited at her hostel, Miss Wellington, a Canadian woman of great courage and with a great sense of mission, and questioned her, saying, when they released her, that they would return the next morning…. The member of the consular staff who went to Miss Wellington at 6 a.m. the next morning found that she had already been taken away. Troutbeck and I spent the morning going from one branch of the Gestapo to another without success. She had in fact been taken by the dreaded Sicherheitsdienst and was not released to us till 12.30 p.m. after hard grilling, but with no physical ill-treatment. She was exhausted but still full of courage.*

According to Warriner,

> *They questioned her for six hours, making her stand all the time. It was a different set of Gestapo, the SD, [This was Himmler's intelligence police, which was declared a criminal organization at the Nuremberg trials] evidently wild about the refugee work. She stood up to them splendidly: they got not a step further. They asked her where the British Legation*

was, and she said "Look in the phone book." They accused
her of illegal activities, and she said, "Everything that you
do is illegal".....From this experience, she emerged much
exhausted, but in an exalted mood.

One might wonder about the bravura answers that Wellington gave to the S.D. She was, of course, the only witness, but as other incidents will bear out, she was very pugnacious and never shrank from confrontation, so maybe there is an element of truth in her account of the interrogation. The consulate strongly advised her to go home after this experience but, in Stopford's words, she "flatly refused our attempts to get her to leave Prague".

A week after Wellington's adventures with the Gestapo, Doreen Warriner herself had to leave Prague as we saw in Chapter One. Now, with Warriner, Maxwell and Dougan all gone, there was really only one person with the drive and the knowledge to take the BCRC rescue work forwards. In Warriner's words, "In spite of her ordeal, Beatrice Wellington was quite ready to take over my work, and since then has dealt directly with von Boemelberg, getting exit permits for the remainder of the women."

These were increasingly difficult times for the new head of the BCRC, especially one who does not seem to have had a gift for diplomacy and compromise. Sponsors in England were drying up and the Committee was running out of money; there were plans to phase out the present organization and replace it with the CRTF, the Czech Refugee Trust Fund which would be similar to the BCRC but under more government control; a new man, Walter Creighton, was coming out to Prague as a partial replacement for the brilliant Stopford. The Gestapo were gradually closing off the trade in illegals via the railway to Poland; the Prague Institute, with the encouragement of the Nazis, were trying to take over responsibility for all Jewish emigration and both were eager to limit the work of the English aid agencies. But for Wellington, all these obstacles were secondary to her "mission" which was to get the remaining women and children on her Lists out of the country.

What she must have realised very quickly was that if she was going to fulfill this goal then it would be wisest to put her arguments with the Gestapo behind her and follow all the rules. Parts of a lengthy document addressed to The BCRC back in London is worth quoting because it shows not only what her values and priorities were, but also that she was prepared to deliver what amounts to a moral lecture to the committee about its obligations. This also gives us some insight into the sort of person she was. She begins by listing, in point form, "the scope of the work since the last transport, May 20, 1939". The first requirement is "to clear as far as possible the HOME OFFICE LIST as at present constituted." On the matter of fulfilling promises already made to refugees she writes:

> *I am assuming the Committee will continue to take very seriously their responsibility in regard to any commitment made by Miss Warriner as their representative, and unavoidably left unfulfilled by her. As her successor in a temporary capacity, I am convinced of my own moral responsibility to urge that the Committee attend to these obligations if not before, certainly at the same time as they take on others, and I am equally sure of the necessity, for the sake of the future work of the Committee in Czechoslovakia, of leaving no stone unturned to see that in the matter of old commitments, there is a clean slate as far as the international situation will permit the fulfilment of undertakings.*

This is all by the way of an introduction to what appears to be the main thrust of her long memorandum - an attack on the whole policy of aiding the escape of "illegals" via the underground railway to Poland. This, of course, was one of Warriner's favourite projects:

> *The Committee has, by aiding men who arrived in Poland, greatly increased its own liabilities here as regards the women and children who remain, and who are without food and shelter. They have placed upon their worker here [i.e., herself] a moral responsibility which she cannot neglect, and which she can fulfill by giving aid to these women only at the risk of expulsion from this country and cessation of the Committee's work by order of the existing authority. It has already been made clear to me by the Gestapo that the British Committee Representative here, regardless of who he or she is, will be promptly expelled from the country, if found attempting to aid the women and children of men who have got to Poland illegally, and are now in England or en route to England, as a result of the activities of the Committee representative in Poland, which are now well known in Berlin.*
>
> *A greater disaster resulting from this policy is that the cause of the women and children themselves has been menaced, and to date an increasing number of women are being imprisoned, or are being subjected to mental torture, because the records show that their husbands have been aided in Poland.*

She is obviously indignant that the Polish escape routes are in danger of undermining, if not destroying, the work she is doing legitimately in Prague, and she ends her memorandum to London with what can only be termed impertinence.

> *CONCLUSION.... If the Czech people still are the major interest of the Committee, and if the Committee still*

wishes to operate under its present title, the most detrimental thing they can continue to do, is to attempt to beat the Gestapo at their own game, and expect a representative of the Committee to meet with any degree of co-operation from that body in Prague. The policy is unsound from the standpoint of organizational integrity, from the standpoint of financial negotiations, from the standpoint of humanitarian motives, and from the standpoint of the ultimate purpose of the Committee.

This letter reflects Wellington's state of mind in May/June of 1939, and ominously the situation was only going to get more difficult for her in June/July as war got closer and she desperately tried to get exits permits for her refugee families from the Gestapo. Margaret Layton wrote to her urging her to take a holiday, and offering her almost any job with the BCRC in London that appealed to her.

When you come back here in June I expect you will want a holiday to recover from your very strenuous labours especially as I gather that you have not been in very good health lately. But when you are rested we should be very glad if you would continue to work for our Committee in some capacity or other....

Later she received an urgent telegram asking her to return to London for a meeting, but she refused to go because, as she said, she had "doubts as to the motive of recall".

But London were not the only ones who were finding Wellington a difficult person to handle. In Stopford's words:

As time went on, the Germans became more and more resentful of the position which Miss Wellington had made for herself, while she, seeing the shadows closing in, became more and more determined to force the Refugee Institute and the Gestapo to do what she wanted with regard to all the refugees in whom she was interested....She became more and more convinced that she had a "mission" which could only be carried out by being tough with the Gestapo....The Kriminalrat [von Boemelberg] was not a strong Nazi and was anxious to co-operate as far as he could with us, but could not be seen to be yielding to pressure. As time went on, he told Creighton that he was tired of Miss Wellington's methods and begged him to get her withdrawn.... Miss Wellington, however, remained in Prague.

Obviously her tactics were to turn up at Boemelberg's office every day, and make her demands with a steely persistence bordering on aggressiveness. This seems to have had the desired results. Whether one should go so far as to imagine a situation where it is the Gestapo who are being browbeaten is questionable, but it is not too far-fetched to suggest that exit permits were signed rather more quickly in the hopes of getting rid of her.

On July 31 there was an article in The Daily Telegraph that claimed she had been deported from Prague by order of the Gestapo. The story was picked up by the Vancouver papers ("Nazi Police Drive City Ex-Teacher Out Of Prague") which added that Vincent Massey, the Canadian High Commissioner, had requested an official explanation. Wellington herself wrote, with characteristic bluntness, a refutation that began:

With reference to a statement appearing in the "Daily Telegraph" of Monday, July 31, 1939 concerning the interruption of the work in Prague of the British Committee for Refugees from Czechoslovakia and referring to my departure from Prague "upon the order of the Gestapo", I feel the necessity of making the following statement: That the entire content of the article is incorrect....

The first third of her article consists of an analysis of the behaviour of Pettit, the British Vice-Consul in Prague, and what a devious and ineffective man he is. In the final third she launches into an attack on her bête noir, Walter Creighton, the man who had been sent out to supervise, if not replace her. He was someone, she begins by saying, "whose exact function in Prague always remained a mystery". She then goes on to describe how he would pass on to her the annoyance of the Gestapo about some action or other, and how she would then immediately go to the Gestapo to check on the accuracy of this message, and find it untrue. She concludes,

> *The impression that Mr. Creighton gave to those of us who sought his co-operation on specific matters of general policy, in the work in Prague, was that of deep dissatisfaction at having to be in Prague at all, plus a genuine dislike of refugees and all problems relating to them, and a sincere desire to leave Prague as soon as possible and permanently.*

But this was all something of a rearguard action for Wellington. World War II was only four weeks away, and throughout Europe people were closing up shop, and putting shutters on the windows. She had battled long and hard with the authorities, both German and English, on behalf of her refugee families, but it all had to come to an end. She left Prague on August 3rd, 1939. The above document appears to have been written after she got back to England, and it very much appears to be a case of "getting things off her chest", a parting shot. The last two lines make it clear where she laid the blame, not entirely justly, for the mess that she had tried to cope with during the final two months of her rescue efforts:

"whoever may have engineered this move [to close us down] it was not due to local interference or antagonism on the part of the Gestapo, but rather to machinations arranged by British Authorities."

* * *

Back in London, Wellington continued to work for the BCRC/CRTF, according to the Vancouver papers, "acting as interpreter, liaison officer and moral support" for the many refugees she had managed to help escape. One story has it that when she arrived in England, she was met by an irate official of some sort who packed her off to a large centre for Czech refugees on the Isle of Man, and told her to straighten out the mess she had created by issuing such a large number of visas under fictitious names. But she was also still involved with potentially hazardous fieldwork. There is an intriguing Home Office note for May 11, 1940 from the director of the CRTF to her saying:

> *Your forthcoming visit to France for the purpose of facilitating the evacuation of a body of refugees from Sudetenland hitherto living in Belgium....is undertaken with the approval of the Czech Refugee Trust.*

Doreen Warriner was scheduled to accompany her. Presumably these were some of their former clients who had got as far as Belgium, and were still trying to keep one step ahead of the Germans. Documents tell us that Warriner cancelled her journey at the last minute. It is not recorded what Wellington did, but she probably did likewise. It was two weeks before Dunkirk.

There is another letter in the National Archives from a certain E.N. Cooper of the Home Office that indicates that during these war years Wellington continued to provoke admiration and annoyance in equal measure:

> As regards Miss Wellington, she is the victim of refugee intrigues which, I think, are still persisting. I distrust the intriguers and distrust the motives behind their intrigues. If your enquiry means that Miss Wellington's employment in refugee work is considered undesirable, I would ask you first to consult Inspector Crane of the Special Branch and secondly let me know why you think so.
>
> I may add that at present Miss W. is working under Miss Bertha Bracey in the German Emergency Committee, and that Miss Bracey has the highest opinion of her, as have I.

As the war drew to an end she was, in the words of her brother, Dr. W.G. Wellington,

> drawn more and more into agencies that began to grow up around the projected idea of a United Nations. As soon as the war ended, she was off to Poland to help organize various aspects of post-war relief under the auspices of UNRA, (the United Nations relief organization).

She was there until nearly 1948, when she became seriously ill with typhoid and was invalided home. She worked for a time at the United Nations in New York, and was in line for a permanent job which some say was as a secretary to Lester Pearson when he was chairman of one of the many U.N. committees, or perhaps when he was President of the General Assembly. However, when a security check was run on her it was discovered that her real name was Gonzales, because her stepfather had never legalized the name change. She lost the job. It is possible that this disappointment and her fragile health caused a breakdown, and she spent some time in hospital, including a psychiatric ward. Eventually she returned to the Canadian West and taught in the public school systems of Alberta and British Columbia.

Her last job was at Eastglen Composite High School in Edmonton. It was here that one winter day she cut her foot on a piece of glass. The cut became septic, gangrene developed and, in a strange echo of Trevor Chadwick's final days, she had to have the leg amputated. Unfortunately this wound didn't heal, perhaps due to some form of diabetic condition, and she lapsed into a coma and died on April 7th, 1971. When she died a colleague wrote the following letter to her brother:

The students whom your sister taught were visibly moved when I told them of her passing. Even during the two weeks when she was in a coma, many students stopped me in the halls and asked for her. High school children are strange: they can give the teacher a difficult time, but when sickness strikes they are very solicitous. One boy who was a particular thorn in the flesh actually wept when I broke the news to him privately. I think all the students knew they were being taught English by a very special person but, being children, they wouldn't admit it but preferred to giggle and whisper and complain. It was a case of the generation gap being just too wide, and there was little I could do to help matters.

Your sister was not really happy with us at Eastglen nor with the people at Central Office. She would say we didn't try to help, but believe me , we did. She told none of us she was suffering from diabetes. We knew she was not well, but we couldn't get the facts because somehow we could not get her to have an adequate medical examination..... We now feel that she was afraid of the medical because it would probably cost her her job. We realize, too, that her condition was responsible for her having many bad days and some very good ones.... I am writing this, Dr. Wellington, because I want you to know that we tried to help your sister, but I'm afraid we failed. If word has reached you that we did nothing, it is not true. We did what we could despite some very difficult days. I liked Miss Gonzales and only wish that I had known her in her prime. We had many laughs together and exchanged many stories about teaching. I am enclosing a card from her students and also the signatures (97) of all the people she taught at Eastglen.

Dr. Wellington replied:

Thank you so much for your letter of May 5th. I enclose a reply to Beatrice's students – an expression of my own family's gratitude which I hope you will show them. But this letter that I am sending along with that reply is for you. My wife and I are grateful for the thoughts expressed in your letter, and we want you to know that we are not casting about for someone to blame. If funerals must happen, we prefer a remembering, not a recriminatory aftermath.

We did not know beforehand that Beatrice had diabetes. Neither, do we think did she know. But the diabetes proved controllable, so we doubt that the problems that seem to have arisen over the medical exam were due to fear of discovery. If you had had time to know her better, you would have soon discovered that the attitude toward authority that made her flout the Nazis in Czechoslovakia recurred in diverse forms. So please don't let speculation replace her life-long disrespect for constituted authority with mere fear of job loss. Let them leave her her rebelliousness. In the letter to the students, I mentioned that Beatrice saved many refugees from arrest and imprisonment by the Gestapo just before the war. Because of those acts my wife and I donated to an international fund that plants memorial groves in Israel. The students might wish to remember the epitaph. We wrote: "She practiced humanity when others would not."

These letters constitute a fitting summary of Wellington's difficult and restless life. Her great achievement was to help hundreds of people to safety in 1939. We may therefore end with the final words from Doreen Warriner's memoir *The Winter in Prague.*

When I got back to England Beatrice Wellington kept me advised by telegram of what was happening. One large party left early in May across Germany. On May 22nd, I went to Liverpool Street to meet the last of the women who had been in my charge. Beatrice Wellington stayed on in Prague, dealing with the remaining women, and did not return to England until the end of July, by which time she had got them all out.

EPILOGUE

Loose ends..... It might be assumed that the five people featured in this story all came out of the same box, the one marked "good Samaritan", and to a large extent this is true. They all witnessed people in distress and, without hesitation, dropped what they were about to do - a skiing holiday, scholarly research, a teaching job, and for a few months devoted themselves to saving as many of the dispossessed as they could. What is equally striking, however, is, apart from the Good Samaritan gene, how different they all were; different in their professions, different in their personalities, and different in the trajectories that their later lives took. When they all came together in 1939, one was a banker, one was a university lecturer, one a teacher, a lifeboat crewman and ex-colonial officer, one was with the Y.W.C.A., and the fifth was himself a refugee. Later, two had fairly conventional careers in the business world and at a university; for a third, life fell apart for a few years, and he slowly had to re-discover himself in a foreign country; a fourth was cursed (or blessed) with "a sense of mission", and in a world that often failed to conform to her standards, brought both discomfort as well as comfort to herself and others.

We should emphasize here again that though Doreen Warriner, Nicholas Winton, Trevor Chadwick and Beatrice Wellington were the ones who (with the help of R.J. Stopford) spear-headed the British (and Canadian) efforts in Prague, and are the subject of this book, there were a great many others both from England and from other countries, and indeed from Czechoslovakia itself, for example the Czech Refugee Institute, who played a crucial role in the rescue efforts. Planes and trains and boats took refugees to France and Switzerland and Israel and Sweden, and, crucially, to Canada which agreed to take over one thousand families.

It is also worth noting that in Prague, at what we might call the rough end of the rescue operation, where life for the rescuers must have been exhausting, and emotionally draining, and sometimes a little bit frightening especially after the Germans arrived, it appears to have been women who did the lion's share of the work, Warriner and Wellington, of course, who led the British effort, but also the latter's colleagues, Miss Wilson and Miss Rogers, and Warriner's main assistants, Margaret Dougan and Christine Maxwell, who accompanied trains and did secretarial work, as did Tessa Rowntree and her cousin Jean. Then there were the two Czech girls, Ruth Reser and her friend, who worked for Chadwick in the Children's Section office, and Hilde Patz whom Warriner called "one of the best workers I had ever known," and many more Czech women: Emma Goerlich, Emmi Dolling, Frau Schnabel and Schmolka, and so on. It was, of course, more hazardous for the Czechs to help. Emma Goerlich ended up in Ravensbruck.

It is probably true that, as Dogberry in *Much Ado About Nothing* says, comparisons are odorous, but it is also interesting to wonder why there is such a wide discrepancy in the honours and prestige awarded to the five people we have been considering. As we know, Winton received a knighthood, and has been honoured with awards and statues in many countries. His is an exemplary life, and these rewards for his great achievement with the Kindertransports may stand as a benchmark. Warriner received an O.B.E. for her work which is a much less resounding gong, and she herself is not at all well known. Perhaps this is an effect of longevity, but we should remember that she was directly responsible for saving at least four or five times the number of people than were saved by the Kindertransports, and that a large percentage of those were children and/or Jews. Posterity is not an even-handed dispenser of esteem. Then there is Chadwick who was not officially acknowledged, though there was a longish article in the Review section of The Observer, ten years after his death, under the somewhat melodramatic headline, "The Pimpernel of Prague", and Barazetti who was immensely over-acknowledged with Yad Vashem's honorific title of Righteous Among the Nations. But it seems to me that it is the Canadians who come closest to making the appropriate gesture. Wellington's family endowed the Beatrice Wellington Gonzales Memorial Scholarship at the University of British Columbia. It commemorates "her strenuous and successful efforts to protect and salvage the lives of political refugees in Europe prior to and during World War II. In making this award, special consideration will be given to students who like Miss Gonzales are concerned about the plight of individuals." Perhaps such a memorial scholarship, awarded afresh each year to a young student, keeps the flame alight more effectively than the rather ephemeral English titles and medals.

And as a footnote to this history of those who made the evacuation of refugees from Prague possible, we should add the splendid affirmation of Hugo Marom, himself a former Kind, that the real heroes of the transports were the parents. It is a measure of their love and their courage that they were prepared to hand their children over to total strangers, to be carried to countries they'd never visited, to be looked after by people they'd never met, and who spoke a language they didn't understand. With grim aptness he adds that this was "long before mobile telephones!". To conjure up what the scenes must have been like on the platforms of Masaryk or Wilson stations is painful. The children, apparently, took it all in their childish strides. For many of them it was exciting, novel, a new adventure. For the parents it was a tragedy. Reports tell us that, as they said goodbye to their children, they tried to maintain the inconsequential chatter that served to camouflage deeper feelings and fears; and then there was the fake cheerfulness, the bright, optimistic comments that were shouted up to the crowded windows. "Don't forget to write!"; "We'll see you very soon", while deep in their beings some knew that this might not be possible. For some the anguish was too much.

A fine bronze statue of Sir Nicholas Winton has recently been erected on the platform of Wilson station. Though it might be argued that this statue has a symbolic justification, it is misconceived if it is supposed to be historically accurate. As we have seen, Sir Nicholas probably never set foot on the platforms of this station, and the child he holds was not one of his children. Ideally the statue should have been placed at Liverpool St. station in London, where it could join the lovely group of bronze children with their suitcases. This was Winton's area of operation, meeting the trains as they arrived from mainland Europe, and seeing the children onwards to their foster families.

But by now the myth of the one-man operation is too deeply embedded to be shifted. In the recent stories about the 2009 "Winton Train", the air waves and the print media were clogged with references to "the British Schindler", though it must be said that one or two papers confessed that Winton did not like the comparison. In the end I suppose we are reduced to creating a fantasy memorial of our own for the Prague stations, one that adheres to historical truth, and tells the true story, and one that commemorates not simply the hundreds who went on the Kindertransports, but the thousands of others, many of them also children, many of them Jewish, who escaped to freedom from these stations through the total dedication of the aid workers who quite literally went face to face with the Gestapo on behalf of their charges on these very platforms. In my imagined memorial, the group is headed by two women. The one in front looks cheerful and welcoming; the one slightly behind her is sterner and has a crusading chin. On the plinth on which they stand there are the names of those who also played such an important part in this marvellous rescue effort, Margaret Dougan and Christine Maxwell and Ruth Reser and Hilde Patz, and all the others. And somewhere towards the back, I think I would like to see a tall Englishman. He has a slight smile on his face and, rather surprisingly, he wears a fisherman's jersey. He holds a book which seems to be in Latin. One can just make out the inscription: *Nam homo proponit, sed Deus disponit.*

ACKNOWLEDGEMENTS

The two main acknowledgements are for my brother, Charles Chadwick, and Henry Warriner, Doreen's nephew.

The former did most of the spadework for this book over a number of years. Three fat files containing his correspondence and the results of his archival digging were the rather daunting beginnings for my own researches.

Henry has, first of all, given permission for me to quote extensively from his aunt's splendid memoir *A Winter in Prague*. This is a work that deserves greater recognition. Henry is also something of an expert at digging out information from the National Archives at Kew. He gave me much invaluable information not only about his aunt, but also about Barazetti and Wellington.

Michael Munk who sent a long letter about how Beatrice Wellington helped his family to escape from Prague.

The trustees of the Imperial War Museum for allowing access to Mr. R.J. Stopford's papers and for giving permission to quote from them.

The curator of the Winton papers at the Yad Vashem archives in Jerusalem.

Others who have read parts of the manuscript and made valuable comments are, Jonathan Chadwick, formerly secretary of the Imperial War Museum, Arnold Raphael, the master of Stathe House, and Margret Wellington the sister-in-law of Beatrice, who let me see some pertinent family documents.

Also my son, Robin who did some useful digging in various European archives.

Special mention must go to the poet Gerda Mayer, one of the Kinder, who contributed much crucial information to the early files.

And to my wife, Jackie, who is able to make sure that feet are firmly planted.

BIBLIOGRAPHY

Davidson, Lucy V. For a Future and a Hope. CWI Publications, 1989.

The Encyclopedia of the Righteous Among the Nations: Europe (Part I) and Other Countries. Yad Vashem, Jerusalem, 2007.

Gissing, Vera and Muriel Emanuel. Nicholas Winton and the Rescued Generation. Vallentine Mitchell, 2002.

Gershon, Karen. We Came As Children. Gollancz, 1966.

The Mail on Sunday. "Despair of Britain's Unsung Schindler", November 21, 1999.

The National Archives, Kew. The main files for this study were: HO 294/38,50,53,54,216,554,612,636, and HO 405/3688.

The London Observer. "The Pimpernel of Prague", Sunday, July 10 1988.

Schlesinger, Joe. Time Zones; A Journalist in the World. Random House of Canada, 1991.

R.J. Stopford Papers. Held in the archives of the Imperial War Museum.

The Times. "Bill Barazetti; Obituary", Monday October 9, 2000.

Warriner, Doreen. <u>A Winter in Prague</u>. Ms held at the Imperial War Museum archives. Also published in SEER, Vol 62, No 2, April 1984.